I0116747

Good and Evil

Philosophy of Ethics: The Series, Book 1

L. R. Caldwell

Reason and Reality Publishing

Good and Evil: Philosophers from the Past and Their Views

Copyright © 2025 by L. R. Caldwell

Published by Reason and Reality Publishing

ISBN: 979-8-9992710-3-7

Orcid: 0009-0005-6487-9274

Printed in the United States of America

First Edition: 2025

Dedication

For my beloved parents

Ronald L. Caldwell (1939–2012)
and
Virginia (Sue) Caldwell (1942–2014)

With deepest love, respect, and gratitude.

Plato

Biography

Plato (c. 427–347 BCE) was a Greek philosopher, student of Socrates, and teacher of Aristotle. Born into an aristocratic Athenian family and shaped by the Peloponnesian War and the trial and execution of Socrates (399 BCE), he turned to philosophy as a path to truth and justice.

He founded the Academy in Athens—often regarded as the first institution of higher learning in the Western world—where mathematics, dialectic, and statesmanship formed the core of education. His dialogues explore metaphysics, ethics, politics, and epistemology and have influenced philosophy, theology, and education for millennia.

Summary of Views on Good & Evil

Plato on the Good

Plato elevates the Good above all else because it unites truth, beauty, and justice in a single principle. Only the philosopher who ascends to knowledge of the Good is truly equipped to lead—hence the ideal of the philosopher-king.

In the Republic, the Good is said to be "beyond being in dignity and power" (509b–c), the source of both truth and existence. The Divided Line (509d–511e) distinguishes levels of cognition from opinion to understanding of Forms, culminating in knowledge of the Good. The pedagogical program—arithmetic, geometry, harmonics, astronomy, and dialectic—reorients the soul from appearances to intelligible structure (521d–534e).

Plato also intimates a cosmological dimension to the Good. In the Timaeus (29e–30a), the world's craftsman acts "because he was good," seeking to make the cosmos as good as possible by imposing rational order on pre-existing, disorderly materials. Yet he acknowledges resistance to perfect order: Necessity (ananke) and the "wandering cause" introduce a countervailing factor (47e–48a; 52d).

For Plato, education is teleological: all studies aim at a final vision that integrates knowledge under the Good. In the Symposium (210a–212b) and Phaedrus (249d–250c), eros is redirected from love of particular beauties to contemplation of Beauty itself, refining desire into a striving for what is highest. Politically, a well-ordered soul mirrors a well-ordered polis; only those who have apprehended the Good can rule wisely (Republic IV 435b–444e; VI 503c–504e).

Plato on Evil

Plato treats evil not as an independent principle but as ignorance, disorder, and excess relative to proper measure. In the Philebus (64e–66a) and Statesman (283e–284c), he associates the good with limit and proportion and the bad with the unmeasured and excessive. Socratic claims that "no one errs willingly" are integrated with a tripartite psychology in which reason, spirit, and appetite can conflict (Protagoras 345c–e; Republic 436b–441c).

Culture can corrupt or cure: because imitation reshapes character, permissive poetry and spectacles that reward vice train the soul to love appearances rather than truth (Republic II–III 377a–403c; X 595a–608b). The Cave allegory (VII 514a–517a) shows how evil thrives through illusion and complacency, when people prefer shadows to knowledge. In political life, tyranny is the fullest manifestation of collective evil (Republic VIII 562a–569c; IX 571a–576b).

At root, wrongdoing stems from ignorance—mistaking lesser goods (wealth, pleasure, honor) for the ultimate Good. Hence the remedy for evil is education that corrects false opinions and restores proper psychic order, with reason ruling over spirit and appetite.

Influences on Plato's Views of Good and Evil

• Political turmoil in Athens: the Peloponnesian War, the regime of the Thirty (404–403 BCE), the restoration of democracy, and the trial of Socrates (399 BCE) informed Plato's skepticism about unbridled popular rule and civic ignorance.

• Sophistic culture and rhetoric: professional teachers of persuasion prompted Plato's critique of rhetoric that seeks victory rather than truth (Gorgias), and his insistence that speech be disciplined by knowledge of the good.

• Pythagorean mathematics and harmony: contact with Archytas and Pythagoreanism reinforced Plato's conviction that reality has an intelligible, mathematical structure and that education must turn the soul toward stable objects of knowledge.

• Eleatic monism and the challenge of change: engagement with Parmenides pressed Plato to clarify the status of unchanging Forms vis-à-vis the world of becoming (Parmenides).

• Experiments in statesmanship: Plato's Sicilian efforts (narrated in the Seventh Letter, authenticity debated) tempered optimism about the ease of reforming power from within.

Three Modern Questions & "Likely" Responses

• Misinformation and "fake news": Plato would see misinformation as a corruption of truth that keeps people in the Cave; he would call for education that elevates souls toward the Good and for leaders oriented to wisdom rather than power.

• Consumerism and material excess: he would diagnose rampant appetite overwhelming reason and urge a restoration of psychic order and civic education in virtue.

• Artificial intelligence: like rhetoric in Gorgias, technology can either elevate truth or manipulate the many; what matters is whether it is guided by reason and justice toward the Good.

Simplified Summary

Plato held that the Good is the highest reality—like the sun that makes knowledge possible. Evil is ignorance and inner disorder, when appetite overrules reason. People often live in "caves" of illusion; education and philosophy lift us toward wisdom, justice, and harmony. In simple terms, Plato believed that to live well, we must train both our minds and our desires toward what is truly lasting and real. For him, philosophy was not just a subject to study, but a way of life—a lifelong effort to leave the shadows of ignorance and to align ourselves with truth, justice, and harmony in both personal character and public life.

References (Primary Sources)

Plato. Complete Works. Edited by John M. Cooper and D. S. Hutchinson. Indianapolis: Hackett, 1997. (Includes G. M. A. Grube/C. D. C. Reeve, Republic; Donald J. Zeyl, Timaeus; H. N. Fowler, Symposium.)

Plato. Republic. Benjamin Jowett, trans. Public-domain online editions used for spot-checking passages (e.g., MIT Internet Classics).

Plato. Phaedrus. David Horan, trans., Platonic Foundation (online).

Plato. Seventh Letter (authenticity debated).

References (Secondary & Web Sources)

Annas, Julia. An Introduction to Plato's Republic. Oxford: Clarendon Press, 1981.

Irwin, Terence. Plato's Ethics. Oxford: Oxford University Press, 1995.

Kraut, Richard, ed. The Cambridge Companion to Plato. Cambridge: Cambridge University Press, 1992.

Reeve, C. D. C. Philosopher-Kings: The Argument of Plato's Republic. Princeton: Princeton University Press, 1988.

Sedley, David. "The Ideal of Godlikeness." In Plato 2: Ethics, Politics, Religion, and the Soul, ed. Gail Fine, 309–328. Oxford: OUP, 1999.

Vlastos, Gregory. Socrates: Ironist and Moral Philosopher. Ithaca, NY: Cornell University Press, 1991.

Frede, Dorothea. "Plato's Ethics: An Overview." Stanford Encyclopedia of Philosophy (accessed Sept. 13, 2025).

Brown, Eric. "Plato: ethics and politics in The Republic." Stanford Encyclopedia of Philosophy (accessed Sept. 13, 2025).

Griswold, Charles L. "Plato on Rhetoric and Poetry." Stanford Encyclopedia of Philosophy (accessed Sept. 13, 2025).

Huffman, Carl A. "Pythagoreanism" (and "Archytas"). Stanford Encyclopedia of Philosophy (accessed Sept. 13, 2025).

"Timaeus." Internet Encyclopedia of Philosophy (accessed Sept. 13, 2025).

Public-domain online texts consulted for verification: MIT Internet Classics (Republic), Harvard/BU course PDFs on the Cave (Rep. 514a–517a), Platonic Foundation translations of Republic (509b–511e) and Timaeus (47e–48a).

Further research into Plato's thought has emphasized the continuity between his metaphysical commitments and his political philosophy. Scholars such as Christopher Rowe and Melissa Lane stress that the pursuit of the Good informs not only individual psychology but also institutional design, linking the Republic's educational scheme to broader civic reform.

This line of interpretation situates Plato as less of an abstract metaphysician and more as a social theorist whose ideals, though radical, respond directly to the crises of democratic Athens.

Other commentators have drawn attention to Plato's engagement with earlier Greek traditions, especially tragedy and pre-Socratic cosmology. Martha Nussbaum and Catherine Zuckert argue that Plato's dialogues cannot be fully understood apart from his critical appropriation of tragic motifs and his engagement with Heraclitus, Parmenides, and the Sophists.

These studies underscore the literary and dramatic dimensions of Plato's work, suggesting that his philosophy communicates as much through form and myth as through strict logical argument.

The reception of Plato in late antiquity and beyond also continues to inform contemporary scholarship.

Neoplatonists such as Plotinus and Proclus reinterpreted the Good as the One, integrating Plato with a mystical ascent that profoundly influenced Christian theology, particularly Augustine.

Modern studies of this reception—by Lloyd Gerson and Dominic O'Meara, among others—highlight the enduring theological dimension of Platonic thought and its impact on metaphysical traditions across cultures.

Recent debates in analytic philosophy have revived interest in Plato's theory of Forms, with some philosophers exploring whether abstract objects remain indispensable for a coherent account of mathematics, language, and ethics. Figures like Nicholas White and Gail Fine defend the continuing philosophical significance of Platonic realism, while critics question whether Plato's commitment to transcendent entities can be reconciled with modern scientific naturalism. This dialogue keeps Plato at the center of ongoing disputes about realism, idealism, and the nature of value.

Aristotle

Biography

Aristotle (384–322 BCE) was a Greek philosopher and polymath, born in Stagira, a city in northern Greece. He studied at Plato's Academy in Athens for nearly twenty years before founding his own school, the Lyceum. Unlike Plato, who emphasized transcendent Forms, Aristotle grounded his philosophy in the empirical world, seeking to understand nature, logic, ethics, politics, and metaphysics through observation and systematic reasoning. His works, such as the *Nicomachean Ethics*, *Politics*, and *Metaphysics*, remain foundational to Western philosophy. As tutor to Alexander the Great, Aristotle influenced both intellectual and political history. His method stressed categorization, teleology (the idea that everything has a purpose), and the pursuit of knowledge through experience and reason. Over time, his philosophy became a cornerstone of medieval scholasticism and continues to inform discussions of ethics, science, and political theory.

Summary of Views on Good & Evil

Aristotle's conception of good is closely tied to the idea of eudaimonia, often translated as 'flourishing' or 'living well.' For him, the good life is achieved by fulfilling one's natural function (ergon) in accordance with virtue (aretē). Good is not abstract or transcendent, but practical, rooted in the balance of human character and action. He emphasized the 'Golden Mean,' the principle that virtue lies between extremes of excess and deficiency.

For example, courage is the mean between cowardice and recklessness. Thus, good is realized when individuals live in accordance with reason, cultivating virtues that promote harmony within the self and society. Evil, by contrast, emerges when individuals fall into imbalance—choosing extremes or neglecting rational guidance.

Rather than viewing evil as a metaphysical force, Aristotle framed it as the result of poor judgment, vice, or the failure to cultivate virtue. His account integrates ethics with psychology and politics, suggesting that a well-ordered community is essential for nurturing the conditions in which virtue can thrive. (NE I.7, 1097b22–1098a20; II.6, 1106b36–1107a8; VI.5, 1140a24–1140b30; X.6–8, 1176a30–1179a33; Pol. I.1, 1252a1–7; I.2, 1252b27–30).

Aristotle on Good

For Aristotle, the highest human good is eudaimonia—often translated as flourishing or living well—understood not as a feeling but as a life-long activity of the soul in accordance with virtue. He argues from the 'function' (ergon) of a human being: since our distinctive capacity is rational activity, the good life must be the excellent exercise of reason.

This makes eudaimonia an activity (energeia), not a possession, and it explains why character (ethos) and habituation are central: virtues dispose us to choose well consistently over time in changing circumstances (NE I.7, 1097b22–1098a20; II.1, 1103a14–26).

Virtue (aretē) is a mean relative to us, discovered by the practically wise person (phronēsis). Aristotle's account of the mean does not promote mediocrity; rather, it identifies the calibrated excellence between deficiency and excess with respect to passions and actions.

Courage, for instance, is the mean between cowardice and rashness; temperance steers between insensibility and self-indulgence. The mean is set 'by reason and as a prudent person would set it,' so its placement depends on the particulars of a life well led (NE II.6, 1106b36–1107a8; VI.5, 1140a24–1140b30).

Because human beings are political and social by nature, the good life unfolds within relationships and institutions. Friendship (philia) is not an optional adornment but a requirement for living well, since friends help us exercise virtue, judge ourselves truly, and share in rational activity together.

Likewise, the city (polis) exists 'for the sake of living well,' aiming at the highest common good. Thus, ethical formation and civic order interlock: laws educate character, while virtuous citizens sustain just laws (NE VIII.1, 1155a3–5; Pol. I.1, 1252a1–7; I.2, 1252b27–30; III.9, 1280b6–10). (see also NE VIII.1, 1155a5–6)

Aristotle is neither a puritan nor a hedonist about goods. External goods, health, friends, sufficient wealth, good birth, even a bit of luck—matter because they supply the material conditions in which virtue can operate effectively; misfortune can impede a noble life.

Still, these are means, not the end. At the pinnacle stands contemplation (theōria), the most continuous, self-sufficient, and god-like activity, which crowns a life already shaped by moral virtue. Practical excellence orders ordinary life; contemplation perfects it (NE I.8–11, 1099a31–1101a14; X.6–8, 1176a30–1179a33).

Aristotle on Evil

Aristotle does not treat evil as a metaphysical rival to good but as moral failure: settled vice (kakia), incontinence (akrasia), and bad choices that deviate from reason.

Vices are stable dispositions opposed to the virtues; they pull us toward excess or deficiency and thereby corrupt judgment and desire. Because character is formed by habituation, we are responsible for becoming the kind of people who find certain actions 'easy' or 'pleasant'—for better or worse (NE II.1, 1103a14–26; II.3, 1104b3–1105a3).

A central analysis of moral failure is akrasia, acting against one's better judgment. The akratic person knows the right principle but is overpowered by appetite or emotion at the moment of choice; the continent person resists this pull. Aristotle dissects how knowledge can be 'inoperative' under passion and how repeated choices sediment into character— either toward virtue or toward vice (NE VII.1–10, 1145b12–1152a35).

Evil also wears civic faces. Injustice, for Aristotle, is not merely breaking a rule but grasping more than one's fair share (pleonexia) and thereby disturbing proportional equality within the community. Because political order aims at the common good, regimes that treat private interest as the highest end are 'deviations'—notably tyranny, which subordinates the city to one person's advantage. These disorders cultivate vice at scale, training citizens to prize domination over virtue (NE V, 1129a1–1138b30; Pol. III.6–7, 1279a22–1279b10).

Responsibility for evil actions turns on voluntariness. Acts done under compulsion or through non-culpable ignorance may be excused, but most wrongdoing stems from choices for which agents are answerable—especially when their ignorance is itself the product of negligence. Because we become just by doing just acts (and unjust by doing unjust acts), Aristotle grounds accountability in the formation of choice (prohairesis) and the will's role in shaping who we are (NE III.1–5, 1109b30–1115a3).

Three Modern Questions & "Likely" Responses
Question 1

Question: How would Aristotle respond to the modern problem of consumerism and material excess?

Aristotle would argue that consumerism represents an excess that disrupts the balance necessary for a virtuous life. According to his principle of the Golden Mean, wealth is not inherently bad but becomes problematic when pursued without limit or disconnected from higher purposes.

He would likely say that unchecked consumerism encourages vice—such as greed and intemperance—by distorting priorities and fostering imbalance. A virtuous approach would require moderation, using wealth and possessions not as ends in themselves but as means to support human flourishing and rational self-development. (NE IV.1–2, 1120a1–1122a34; Pol. I.8–10, 1256b27–1258b9; NE I.5, 1096a5–10).

Question 2

Question: What would Aristotle say about the challenges of mental health in contemporary society?

Aristotle would interpret mental health challenges through the lens of harmony and imbalance within the soul. He saw human well-being as dependent on the proper cultivation of virtues and rational control over passions. If emotions dominate reason, disorder and suffering follow. He would likely recommend practices that promote balance, such as habits of moderation, reflection, and community life, as means of restoring harmony.

While modern medicine adds biological explanations, Aristotle's framework highlights the importance of nurturing psychological resilience and moral character as foundations for health. He would stress the role of family, friendship, and civic life in supporting individuals, since virtue and flourishing are inseparable from community. (NE II.1–3, 1103a14–1105a3; VI.5, 1140a24–1140b30; VIII.1, 1155a3–5).

Question 3

Question: How would Aristotle approach the ethical dilemmas posed by artificial intelligence?

Aristotle would approach artificial intelligence by asking whether it contributes to or undermines human flourishing. He would not frame AI as inherently good or evil but would evaluate its role in promoting balance and virtue.

If AI serves as a tool that enhances rational activity, frees time for meaningful pursuits, and strengthens community, then it aligns with the good. However, if it fosters dependency, weakens moral responsibility, or encourages excess—such as laziness or the erosion of human judgment—then it would be considered harmful.

Aristotle's emphasis on the Golden Mean suggests that AI must be integrated in moderation, guided by prudence (phronēsis), to ensure it contributes to the flourishing of both individuals and society. (NE I.2, 1094a27–1094b11; VI.4–5, 1140a1–1140b30; Pol. I.1, 1252a1–7).

Comparison of Plato and Aristotle on Good and Evil

Plato and Aristotle share the conviction that the study of ethics concerns the highest human good, yet they diverge in method and substance. Plato locates the Good in a transcendent Form that illuminates all other realities; Aristotle grounds the good in the practical functioning of human nature.

For Plato, the Good is apprehended through dialectic and contemplation of eternal truths; for Aristotle, it is realized through habituation and rational activity in everyday life (Plato, *Republic* VI, 508e–509b; Aristotle, NE I.7, 1097b22–1098a20).

On the question of evil, Plato tends to define wrongdoing as ignorance or lack of knowledge—the soul errs because it does not see clearly the Form of the Good. Aristotle, by contrast, emphasizes moral weakness (akrasia) and vice as failures of habituation and choice, even when some knowledge is present. Evil thus arises not simply from ignorance but from disordered desire and insufficient cultivation of virtue (Plato, *Protagoras* 345c–e; Aristotle, NE VII.1–10, 1145b12–1152a35).

Plato envisions the just society as one governed by philosopher-kings who, having grasped the Good, order the polis according to its vision. Aristotle, though valuing contemplation, insists that the city's purpose is to foster flourishing among ordinary citizens, who cultivate virtue through laws and friendships.

Political structures thus carry different weights: Platonic politics is hierarchical and idealistic, while Aristotelian politics is empirical and oriented toward the conditions of virtue (Plato, *Republic* IV, 427d–434c; Aristotle, Pol. I.1, 1252a1–7; III.9, 1280b6–10).

Despite these differences, Aristotle inherits from Plato the belief that goodness is objective, not relative, and that philosophy must guide human life toward truth and order. Both see the cultivation of the soul as central, though Plato emphasizes ascent to the Forms, while Aristotle emphasizes the mean in embodied life.

Their complementary insights—transcendent vision and practical reason—continue to shape debates about morality, politics, and human purpose (Plato, *Republic* VII, 514a–520a; Aristotle, NE II.6, 1106b36–1107a8).

Simplified Summary

Aristotle believed that the good life is about balance, purpose, and living with virtue. He thought that good comes from developing habits of moderation, where courage, honesty, and generosity guide our actions. Evil, for him, was not a mystical force but the result of living out of balance—choosing too much or too little of something important.

He believed that happiness is found when people live in harmony with reason, community, and their natural purpose. Applied to today, Aristotle's philosophy reminds us that problems like greed, stress, or technology misuse can be resolved by seeking moderation and focusing on what truly helps people grow and thrive.

Bibliography

Aristotle. *Nicomachean Ethics*. In The Complete Works of Aristotle: The Revised Oxford Translation, ed. Jonathan Barnes. Princeton: Princeton University Press, 1984.

Aristotle. *Politics*. In The Complete Works of Aristotle: The Revised Oxford Translation, ed. Jonathan Barnes. Princeton: Princeton University Press, 1984.

Aristotle. *Metaphysics*. In The Complete Works of Aristotle: The Revised Oxford Translation, ed. Jonathan Barnes. Princeton: Princeton University Press, 1984.

Plato. *Republic*. In Complete Works, ed. John M. Cooper. Indianapolis: Hackett Publishing, 1997.

Plato. *Protagoras*. In Complete Works, ed. John M. Cooper. Indianapolis: Hackett Publishing, 1997.

Recommended Reading

Aristotle. *Politics*. Translated by Thomas Pangle, 2nd ed. with Peter L. Phillips. Chicago: University of Chicago Press, 2013.

Broadie, Sarah. Ethics with Aristotle. Oxford: Oxford University Press, 1991.

Irwin, Terence. Aristotle's *Nicomachean Ethics*. Indianapolis: Hackett, 1999.

Kraut, Richard. Aristotle: Political Philosophy. Oxford: Oxford University Press, 2002.

Stanford Encyclopedia of Philosophy. "Aristotle's Ethics," "Aristotle's Political Theory," and "Aristotle on Friendship."

Immanuel Kant

Preface:

How to Read Kant's Akademie References

This work uses the standard Akademie edition (Ak) references to Immanuel Kant's writings. These references are universally recognized by scholars and ensure accuracy across different translations. Format: [Abbreviation] [Volume]:[Page number]. Examples: G 4:421 = Groundwork of the Metaphysics of Morals, Volume 4, page 421 in the Akademie edition; KpV 5:110 = Critique of Practical Reason, Volume 5, page 110; R 6:32 = Religion within the Bounds of Bare Reason, Volume 6, page 32. Abbreviations: G = Groundwork of the Metaphysics of Morals; KpV = Critique of Practical Reason; R = Religion within the Bounds of Bare Reason.

Biography
Immanuel Kant (1724–1804) was a German philosopher from Königsberg, East Prussia, whose

work reshaped epistemology, metaphysics, and ethics. Educated and later employed at the University of Königsberg, Kant rarely left his hometown, yet his intellectual reach was vast. Major works include the Critique of Pure Reason (1781/1787), Groundwork of the Metaphysics of Morals (1785), Critique of Practical Reason (1788), and Religion within the Bounds of Bare Reason (1793).

Kant became renowned for his disciplined routine—so regular that townspeople joked they could set their clocks by his afternoon walk. The same internal order informed his philosophy's emphasis on autonomy and lawlike consistency.

Despite his regularity, contemporaries describe Kant as personable and curious. He hosted lively dinner conversations, followed developments in astronomy and natural science, and never married. These habits and interests help explain the union in his thought of moral seriousness with an open, scientific curiosity.

Summary of Views on Good and Evil
Kant grounds goodness in a good will: a will that acts from duty out of reverence for the moral law rather than from inclination or expected consequences. The categorical imperative supplies the supreme principle of morality, requiring universality and respect for persons. Evil, by

contrast, is not mere ignorance or imbalance but a willful subordination of the moral law to self-interest—a propensity Kant calls radical evil. (G 4:393–405; KpV 5:27–30; R 6:32–37).

Kant on Good

The good will is unconditionally good because of its principle: acting from duty in accordance with the moral law. Unlike traits such as courage or intelligence, which can be bent to ill ends, a good will is good in itself. (G 4:393–397).

Kant's most famous statement of the moral law is the Formula of Universal Law: "Act only according to that maxim whereby you can at the same time will that it should become a universal law." (G 4:421).

A complementary statement is the Formula of Humanity: treat humanity, whether in your own person or in any other, always as an end and never merely as a means. (G 4:429–430).

Morality and freedom interlock for Kant: true freedom is autonomy—the self-legislation of rational law—rather than license to follow desire. Practical reason thus reveals our freedom even as it obliges us. (KpV 5:29–33).

Kant's "highest good" (summum bonum) is the envisioned harmony in which virtue is proportionate to happiness. Because this harmony is not guaranteed in the natural order, practical reason postulates God and immortality as conditions that make the highest good intelligible as an object of rational hope. (KpV 5:110–114).

Kant on Evil

Evil originates in the will's decision to prioritize inclination or self-love over the moral law. It is thus a corruption of maxims rather than a mere deficit of knowledge. (R 6:32–37).

In Religion within the Bounds of Bare Reason, Kant argues that humanity has a universal propensity to evil—"radical evil"—that lies at the root of our volition. This propensity does not negate responsibility, because it is rooted in freedom and can be overcome only by a revolution of the heart. (R 6:32–38; 6:47–52).

Kant distinguishes three grades of moral failure: frailty (knowing the law yet failing to follow it), impurity (acting from duty but with mixed motives), and depravity (a fundamental reversal that puts inclination above the law). (R 6:29–33).

Reason itself can be perverted when used to rationalize immoral maxims under universalizable disguises—a particularly insidious form of self-deception. (G 4:424–426).

Kant also stresses that the persistence of evil is tied to the human tendency toward self-deception, where individuals persuade themselves that their actions are morally permissible even when they mask self-interest. This moral distortion is not merely a weakness but reflects reason's ability to fabricate justifications that conceal a reversal of moral priorities. For Kant, the danger of this rationalization lies in its subtlety: once evil is cloaked in the guise of duty or universal law, it becomes harder to expose and correct. Genuine moral reform therefore requires both the recognition of this propensity and a conscious re-ordering of the will, so that the moral law regains unqualified authority over inclination (G 4:424–426; R 6:32–38).

Three Modern Questions and Likely Responses
1. Can morality exist without belief in God?
Kant grounds moral obligation in reason and autonomy, not in divine command. The postulates of God and immortality arise from practical reason's concern with the highest good, not as foundations of duty. Thus morality stands on its own footing, even as rational hope may reach beyond it. (KpV 5:110–114).

2. How does Kant's ethics apply to modern dilemmas?
The Humanity Formula requires that persons never

be treated merely as means. Questions in digital privacy, bioethics, and just war can be assessed by testing maxims for universalizability and by upholding the dignity of rational agents. (G 4:421; 4:429–430).

3. Is "radical evil" still persuasive today?
Kant would allow that environment and psychology influence behavior, yet maintain that responsibility cannot be reduced to them. The notion of a propensity to subordinate the law to self-love explains why wrongdoing can be knowing and deliberate, while preserving the possibility of moral reform. (R 6:32–38; 6:47–52).

Simplified Summary
For Kant, being good depends on why you act, not on what happens afterward. A good will acts from duty and respects rules that anyone could follow. We must also treat people as ends in themselves, never just as tools. Evil happens when we knowingly put self-interest ahead of moral duty—a tendency Kant calls radical evil. Because we are free, we can still change course and realign our lives with the moral law.

Bibliography

Kant, Immanuel. Groundwork of the Metaphysics of Morals. Edited and translated by Mary Gregor. Cambridge University Press, 1998.

Kant, Immanuel. Critique of Practical Reason. Edited and translated by Mary Gregor. Cambridge University Press, 1997.

Kant, Immanuel. Religion within the Bounds of Bare Reason. Edited and translated by Allen Wood and George di Giovanni. Cambridge University Press, 1998.

Kant, Immanuel. Critique of Pure Reason. Edited and translated by Paul Guyer and Allen W. Wood. Cambridge University Press, 1998.

Allison, Henry E. Kant's Theory of Freedom. Cambridge University Press, 1990.

Wood, Allen W. Kant's Ethical Thought. Cambridge University Press, 1999.

Wood, Allen W. Kantian Ethics. Cambridge University Press, 2008.

Korsgaard, Christine M. Creating the Kingdom of Ends. Cambridge University Press, 1996.

Guyer, Paul. Kant on Freedom, Law, and Happiness. Cambridge University Press, 2000.

Appendix: Akademie Edition References

Groundwork of the Metaphysics of Morals
(Grundlegung zur Metaphysik der Sitten): Volume 4
of Ak.

• G 4:393–397 – Introduction of the Good Will.

• G 4:421 – Formula of Universal Law.

• G 4:429–430 – Formula of Humanity.

• G 4:424–426 – On moral self-deception and
universalizability.

Critique of Practical Reason (Kritik der praktischen
Vernunft): Volume 5 of Ak.

• KpV 5:27–30 – Duty and autonomy in moral
action.

• KpV 5:29–33 – Freedom as autonomy of reason.

• KpV 5:110–114 – The Highest Good and the
postulates of God and immortality.

Religion within the Bounds of Bare Reason
(Religion innerhalb der Grenzen der bloßen
Vernunft): Volume 6 of Ak.

• R 6:29–33 – Frailty, impurity, and depravity.

• R 6:32–37 – Evil as corruption of the will.

• R 6:32–38 – Radical evil as universal human propensity.

• R 6:47–52 – Moral reform and the "revolution of the heart".

Suggested Reading

A short, credible list to go deeper on Kant generally and on his treatment of good, evil, and radical evil. Primary texts are given with reliable translations; secondary items are peer-reviewed books or articles.

Primary texts by Kant (reliable translations):

- Immanuel Kant, Groundwork of the Metaphysics of Morals, trans. Mary Gregor; rev. Jens Timmermann (Cambridge University Press, 2011/2012).
- Immanuel Kant, Critique of Practical Reason, trans. Mary Gregor; intro. Andrews Reath (Cambridge University Press, rev. ed.).
- Immanuel Kant, Religion within the Boundaries of Mere Reason, trans. Allen W. Wood & George di Giovanni (Cambridge University Press, 1998/1999).
- Immanuel Kant, The Metaphysics of Morals, trans. Mary Gregor (Cambridge University Press, 1996).

- Immanuel Kant, Lectures on Ethics, ed. & trans. Peter Heath; ed. J. B. Schneewind (Cambridge University Press, 1997).

Secondary scholarship focused on good and evil (books):

- Henry E. Allison, Kant's Theory of Freedom (Cambridge University Press, 1990).
- Allen W. Wood, Kant's Ethical Thought (Cambridge University Press, 1999).
- Paul Guyer, Kant on Freedom, Law, and Happiness (Cambridge University Press, 2000).
- Gordon E. Michalson (ed.), Kant's Religion within the Boundaries of Mere Reason: A Critical Guide (Cambridge University Press, 2014).
- Sharon Anderson-Gold & Pablo Muchnik (eds.), Kant's Anatomy of Evil (Cambridge University Press, 2010).

Targeted journal articles:

- Stephen R. Grimm, "Kant's Argument for Radical Evil," European Journal of Philosophy 10.2 (2002): 160–177.
- Ian McMullin, "Kant on Radical Evil and the Origin of Moral Responsibility," Kantian Review 18.2 (2013): 195–220.

- Matthew Caswell, "The Value of Humanity and Kant's Conception of Evil," Journal of the History of Philosophy 44.4 (2006): 635–663.

Authoritative reference entries (for orientation):

- Robert N. Johnson, "Kant's Moral Philosophy," Stanford Encyclopedia of Philosophy (rev. ed.).
- Lorenzo Pasternack, "Kant's Philosophy of Religion," Stanford Encyclopedia of Philosophy (rev. ed.).

Friedrich Nietzsche

Biography

Friedrich Nietzsche (1844–1900) was a German-born philologist and philosopher whose writings reshaped debates in ethics, culture, psychology, and modern European thought. Born in Röcken, Saxony, Nietzsche studied classical philology at the University of Bonn and later Leipzig before becoming a professor at Basel at the age of twenty-four. Although his academic career was cut short due to ill health, Nietzsche's writings—including *Thus Spoke Zarathustra* (1883–1885), *Beyond Good and Evil* (1886), and *On the Genealogy of Morality* (1887)—reshaped debates in philosophy, psychology, literature, and political theory. He critiqued traditional morality, religion, and metaphysics, pressing for a wholesale revaluation of prevailing values in the wake of what he memorably called the "death of God." Nietzsche's later years were marked by mental illness, leaving him incapacitated until his death in 1900. Despite this, his radical insights into morality, power, and human creativity have continued to resonate, establishing him as a central figure of existential and postmodern thought.

Nietzsche's interest in good and evil arose directly from these personal and intellectual encounters. His fragile health forced him to resign from academia, leaving him to live in relative isolation while writing his most influential works. In this solitude, he turned his attention to how moral values develop and how they either enhance or diminish life. His rejection of inherited moral systems was not abstract speculation alone but a response to both his personal suffering and his observation of European culture in crisis. By tracing how ideas of good and evil arose historically—and how they could be used to regiment human instincts—Nietzsche challenged readers to reassess morality itself and to pursue values grounded in strength, creativity, and self-overcoming.

As a young student, Nietzsche showed extraordinary talent in languages and classical studies, which led him to pursue philology—the study of ancient texts—at the universities of Bonn and Leipzig. His immersion in Greek literature, especially the tragic poets and philosophers, stirred his fascination with questions of suffering, meaning, and the tension between vitality and decline. By the age of twenty-four, he was appointed professor of classical philology at the University of Basel, an exceptional appointment for someone in his early twenties. His deep engagement with ancient culture—particularly its emphasis on strength, creativity, and tragedy—gave him a contrasting lens for thinking about morality outside the confines of Christian doctrine.

Nietzsche's early life played an important role in shaping his philosophical outlook. He was born in 1844 to a Lutheran pastor's family, and his father's death before his fifth birthday left a deep impression on him. Raised largely by his mother and female relatives, he grew up in a strongly religious household, which exposed him to Christian values of humility, obedience, and self-denial. These early experiences helped set the stage for his later critique of Christianity, as Nietzsche came to see traditional morality as a force that both shaped and constrained human life.

Summary of Views on Good and Evil
Nietzsche's reflections on good and evil mark a sharp departure from many earlier philosophical approaches. Rather than seeking universal moral laws or metaphysical foundations, Nietzsche approached morality historically and critically. He distinguished between 'master morality'—arising from the noble, life-affirming values of strength and vitality—and 'slave morality,' which emerged from the resentment (*ressentiment*) of the weak and oppressed. In his view, the concepts of good and evil are not timeless truths but historically

contingent cultural constructs rooted in power struggles and psychological needs. Nietzsche argued that Christian morality, grounded in humility, guilt, and self-denial, exemplified slave morality and distorted human flourishing. By contrast, he called for the revaluation of values and the affirmation of life through creativity, strength, and the ideal of the *Übermensch* (overman). (On the Genealogy of Morality, I.10–13; Beyond Good and Evil, §260–§261; Thus Spoke Zarathustra, Prologue).

Nietzsche on Good

For Nietzsche, the concept of 'good' cannot be understood apart from its historical genesis. In *On the Genealogy of Morality*, he distinguishes between two origins of moral valuation. In master morality, 'good' is identified with strength, nobility, health, and vitality—qualities that affirm life and reflect the self-confidence of powerful individuals and communities. The good is what expresses excellence and superiority. (Genealogy, I.2–I.3).

Slave morality, by contrast, inverts this valuation. For the oppressed, 'good' comes to mean meekness, humility, compassion, and obedience. These values are not expressions of power but strategies of survival, born of *ressentiment*. Here, what was once considered noble or strong becomes labeled 'evil,' while weakness and passivity are praised as 'good.' Nietzsche interprets this inversion as a historical development tied especially to the rise of Christianity. (Genealogy, I.10–I.13).

Nietzsche also critiques the notion of objective or universal goodness. In *Beyond Good and Evil*, he argues that moral concepts are crafted by humans and tend to serve the interests of particular groups or instincts. He calls attention to the 'will to power' as the underlying force that shapes moralities— the drive to assert, expand, and express life. What is considered 'good' is always relative to the perspective and power of those who define it. (Beyond Good and Evil, §260).

The highest expression of good for Nietzsche is found not in conformity to universal rules but in the creation of new values. This task belongs to the *Übermensch*, the figure who overcomes the constraints of inherited morality and affirms life in all its complexity, including suffering. The *Übermensch* embodies self-overcoming, artistic creativity, and a revaluation of values. Goodness, in this sense, is life-affirming power, not obedience to external codes. (Thus Spoke Zarathustra, Prologue §§3–4).

Nietzsche also links the experience of good to aesthetic affirmation. Life, for him, must be justified as an aesthetic phenomenon: to call life 'good' is to embrace it in its fullness, with its chaos, tragedy, and beauty. This aesthetic dimension of good marks a radical departure from earlier moralists, rooting value not in rational law or divine command but in the creative affirmation of existence itself. (The Birth of Tragedy, §24; Thus Spoke Zarathustra, IV.19).

Nietzsche on Evil

For Nietzsche, the concept of 'evil' emerges from the moral inversion characteristic of slave morality. In noble or master morality, there is no strict equivalent of 'evil'; instead, there is a contrast between what is noble (good) and what is base (bad). The concept of 'evil' arises only when the weak, through *ressentiment*, redefine the strong and powerful as evil in order to elevate their own weakness as moral virtue. Thus, evil is not an objective property but a construct born of resentment. (Genealogy, I.10–I.13).

Nietzsche sees Christian morality as the clearest historical example of this process. Christianity, he argues, condemned natural instincts, power, and pride as 'evil' while glorifying meekness, obedience, and suffering as 'good.' This moral inversion, in Nietzsche's view, weakened human vitality and fostered a culture of guilt and self-denial. Evil, then, is not a metaphysical force but the product of a repressive moral system that denies life. (Genealogy, II.4; Beyond Good and Evil, §202).

Nietzsche also critiques the role of guilt in constructing evil. In his genealogy, the concept of guilt (*Schuld*) arose from creditor-debtor relationships, later transformed by religion into moral guilt before God. This transfiguration made human beings see themselves as inherently sinful and evil, burdening them with a debt they could never repay. Such constructions of evil, Nietzsche argues, serve to control populations and suppress instincts. (Genealogy, II.13–II.20).

Evil, in Nietzsche's perspective, is tied to the denial of life and the will to power. Any moral system that suppresses strength, creativity, and affirmation by branding them "evil" risks perpetuating decadence. By contrast, Nietzsche calls for moving 'beyond good and evil'—a revaluation in which categories of good and evil themselves are transcended in favor of life-affirming values. (Beyond Good and Evil, §260–§261).

Finally, Nietzsche emphasizes that clinging to traditional notions of evil perpetuates nihilism. Once belief in God and absolute morality collapses, continued reliance on inherited categories of good and evil leaves humanity directionless. Evil becomes an empty category, a shadow of a moral order that no longer exists. Overcoming this nihilism, Nietzsche argues, requires affirming life without reliance on absolute good and evil and embracing the creative task of value-formation anew. (Thus Spoke Zarathustra, IV.3; Genealogy, III.23–III.25).

Simplified Summary

Nietzsche believed that ideas of good and evil are not universal truths but human inventions shaped by history and power dynamics. He explained that in earlier times, 'good' meant strength, vitality, and creativity, while later, through Christianity and resentment, 'good' came to mean humility and weakness. In this reversal, power and pride were called 'evil,' while meekness was praised as 'good.' Nietzsche thought this shift made people turn against life and their natural instincts. He argued that to truly affirm life, humanity must move 'beyond good and evil'—letting go of old categories and creating new values based on strength, creativity, and self-overcoming. For him, evil was not a supernatural force but a cultural invention used to control people and suppress their vitality.

Bibliography

Nietzsche, Friedrich. *On the Genealogy of Morality*. Edited by Keith Ansell-Pearson.

Translated by Carol Diethe. Cambridge: Cambridge University Press, 2007.

Nietzsche, Friedrich. *Beyond Good and Evil*. Translated by Walter Kaufmann. New York: Vintage, 1989.

Nietzsche, Friedrich. Thus Spoke Zarathustra: A Book for All and None. Translated by Walter Kaufmann. New York: Modern Library, 1995.

Nietzsche, Friedrich. *The Birth of Tragedy and Other Writings*. Edited by Raymond Geuss and Ronald Speirs. Translated by Ronald Speirs. Cambridge: Cambridge University Press, 1999.

Schacht, Richard. *Nietzsche*. London: Routledge, 2013.

Ansell-Pearson, Keith. *An Introduction to *Nietzsche* as Political Thinker: The Perfect Nihilist*. Cambridge: Cambridge University Press, 1994.

Suggested Reading
Nietzsche, Friedrich. *Ecce Homo*. Translated by Walter Kaufmann. New York: Vintage, 1989.

Nietzsche, Friedrich. *Twilight of the Idols*. Translated by Duncan Large. Oxford: Oxford University Press, 1998.

Nietzsche, Friedrich. *The Gay Science*. Edited by Bernard Williams. Translated by Josefine Nauckhoff. Cambridge: Cambridge University Press, 2001.

Young, Julian. *Friedrich Nietzsche: A Philosophical Biography*. Cambridge: Cambridge University Press, 2010.

Clark, Maudemarie. *Nietzsche on Truth and Philosophy*. Cambridge: Cambridge University Press, 1990.

Conway, Daniel W. *Nietzsche's Dangerous Game: Philosophy in the Twilight of the Idols*. Cambridge: Cambridge University Press, 1997.

Gottfried Wilhelm Leibniz

Biography

Gottfried Wilhelm Leibniz (1646–1716) was a German polymath—philosopher, mathematician, diplomat, and jurist—whose work helped shape early modern rationalism alongside Descartes and Spinoza. Born in Leipzig, he studied law and philosophy and later served courts in Mainz, Paris, and Hanover, while corresponding with leading thinkers across Europe. Leibniz independently discovered the differential and integral calculus, designed early calculating machines, and developed a universal language project for science and law. Philosophically, he advanced a systematic metaphysics centered on simple substances (monads), the Principle of Sufficient Reason (PSR), and the doctrine of pre-established harmony. His major texts relevant to ethics and metaphysics include the "Discourse on Metaphysics" (1686), "Monadology" (1714), and the "Theodicy" (1710), as well as essays on justice and happiness collected in standard editions of his philosophical writings. (Leibniz, Monadology §§31–32)

Summary of Views on Good and Evil

Leibniz unifies ethics with metaphysics. Goodness is identified with perfection—degrees of reality and harmony—while evil is a privation or defect relative

43

to such perfection. God, endowed with infinite wisdom and goodness, freely creates the best of all possible worlds—the simplest in hypotheses yet richest in phenomena—where the overall harmony outweighs local defects (Discourse on Metaphysics, §§5–6). (Leibniz, Discourse on Metaphysics §6) Within creation, Leibniz distinguishes three coordinate kinds of good and evil: metaphysical (reality vs. privation), moral (virtue vs. sin), and physical (pleasure vs. pain) (Theodicy, T §209; T §21). Practical reason governs moral conduct through universal principles, the Principle of Sufficient Reason and the Categorical rule to act wisely and charitably—so that justice becomes "the charity of the wise," a love of others guided by reason toward their perfection. Creaturely minds flourish through knowledge of order and the imitation of divine wisdom (Monadology, §§31–32; Leibniz, "Meditation on the Common Concept of Justice"). (Leibniz, Monadology §§31–32) (Leibniz, Natural Law Writings; cf. 'De Justitia et Caritate')

Leibniz on Good

Perfection and Goodness. For Leibniz, the good is not a brute property but the measure of a thing's perfection—its degree of reality, order, and harmony. The metaphysical good is thus co-extensive with being: to be more perfect is to realize a richer unity-in-variety. Because only God is absolutely unlimited, created beings possess limited perfection and therefore some privation. The perfectionist axis of Leibniz's ethics follows: to be good is to increase perfection—first in understanding, then in action—according to reason (Theodicy, T §209; T §21).

PSR and the Architecture of the Good. Leibniz grounds rational evaluation in two master principles: the principle of non-contradiction and the Principle of Sufficient Reason (PSR). The former marks what cannot be; the latter requires that for any truth or fact there is a reason why it is so rather than otherwise (Monadology, §§31–32). PSR links ethics with metaphysics: a wise agent acts by reasons that fit into a wider order, contributing to a maximally coherent plan. Human prudence thus mirrors divine wisdom in choosing the best overall balance of goods. (Leibniz, Monadology §§31–32)

Happiness and Intellectual Pleasure. Leibniz identifies the physical good with pleasure and true happiness with a lasting, stable joy that accompanies the cognition of order. Sensory pleasures are confused perceptions of harmony (as in music), while intellectual pleasures are distinct and enduring. The more we know of the rational structure of reality, the more we participate in happiness; hence, knowledge is not a mere adornment but the very avenue to flourishing (Leibniz, "Felicity").

Virtue and the Charity of the Wise. Moral goodness is virtue, "the habit of acting according to wisdom." Justice, the chief virtue, is defined by Leibniz as the "charity of the wise"—a rational benevolence that wills the perfection and happiness of others for their own sake, while integrating this love into the order of the whole. In practical terms, justice embraces classical legal maxims—do not harm, give each their due, live honorably—reinterpreted through a theistic rationalism that anchors normativity in eternal truths, not arbitrary command (Leibniz, "Meditation on the Common Concept of Justice"; "Codex Iuris Gentium"). (Leibniz, Natural Law Writings; cf. 'De Justitia et Caritate')

The Highest Good and the city-metaphor (sometimes compared to a 'City of God'). God chooses a world that maximizes harmony and value across time—the "best of all possible worlds." For rational creatures, the summum bonum is the convergence of virtue with fitting happiness under a universal moral order.

Leibniz pictures this moral community as a "city-metaphor (sometimes compared to a 'City of God')," a republic of minds governed by wisdom and charity. Human moral progress consists in expanding one's benevolence and insight to align with this divine polity (Discourse on Metaphysics, §6; Monadology, §§83, 85). (Leibniz, Monadology §§84–86)

Freedom and Moral Necessity. Freedom is compatible with foreseen regularity because necessity comes in kinds. Leibniz contrasts "metaphysical" or absolute necessity (e.g., truths of logic) with "moral" or rational necessity, by which a wise will is inclined, without being coerced, to choose the better.

Free agents act from reasons they endorse; such actions can be certain without being fated in the fatalistic sense. This compatibilist account preserves responsibility while embedding choice within PSR-governed order (see Theodicy for the distinction and its application to providence).

Prudence, Law, and the Goods of Community. Because goodness scales with order, law, and custom matter ethically. Good laws educate the will, channeling private aims toward the common good. In Leibniz's natural-law essays, the wise person's charity is universal, extending across nations and times; jurisprudence, ideally, is a science of promoting the best plan for the whole, not merely the advantage of the strong (Leibniz, "Opinion on the Principles of Pufendorf"; "Codex Iuris Gentium").

Leibniz on Evil

Privation, Not Substance. Leibniz interprets evil as a privation—a lack of perfection relative to an ideal—not a positive substance. Because creatures are finite, metaphysical evil (imperfection) cannot be avoided without ceasing to be creatures at all. Evil in this basic sense is the shadow cast by finite being and the necessary contrast that allows a richer harmony overall (Theodicy, T §21).

Three Kinds of Evil. Corresponding to the three kinds of good, Leibniz distinguishes moral evil (sin, vice), physical evil (pain, suffering), and metaphysical evil (privation). Physical and moral evils are permitted—not positively willed—because their inclusion is inseparable from the optimal plan that yields the most order and value in the whole. The presence of lesser ills can be a condition for greater goods—courage, forgiveness, redemption, and the intelligible beauty of a world governed by laws (Theodicy, T §209; T §21).

Best Possible World and the Problem of Evil. Leibniz's theodicy argues that an omniscient, omnipotent, perfectly good God chooses to create the best overall world—"the simplest in hypotheses and the richest in phenomena." A world with no chance for error, struggle, or tragedy might be metaphysically poorer or morally stunted.

What seems "bad in the part" can contribute to maximal goodness in the whole, much as dark patches heighten a painting's overall beauty (Discourse on Metaphysics, §§5–6; Theodicy). (Leibniz, Discourse on Metaphysics §6)

Freedom, Sin, and Responsibility. Moral evil originates in the will's disorder: adopting maxims that prefer partial, short-sighted goods over the hierarchy of goods discerned by reason. Even though God foresees such choices, the agent's act is free because it flows from the agent's own reasons and character, not from external compulsion. Leibniz's "moral necessity" preserves the contingency of free actions while explaining their predictability under complete knowledge (Theodicy).

Mind–Body Appearance and Moral Psychology. In the human case, perceptions and appetitions unfold according to the internal laws of one's monad; no creature truly causes changes in another. Pre-established harmony aligns each substance's states so that bodies and minds run in perfect sync without interaction (Monadology, §§78–81). This framework underwrites a distinctive moral psychology: reform requires inner transformation—

clarifying perceptions and strengthening benevolence—rather than hoping for external causal fixes.

Justice, Punishment, and Mercy. Because justice is the charity of the wise, punishment aims at restoration of order and moral improvement, not mere retribution. Proportionality matters: legal norms should track the true good of persons and communities, discouraging vice while encouraging virtue. Leibniz's jurisprudence thus resists both cruel severity and lax permissiveness, seeking measured responses that promote the harmony of the whole (Leibniz, "Meditation on the Common Concept of Justice"; "Codex Iuris Gentium"). (Leibniz, Natural Law Writings; cf. 'De Justitia et Caritate')

Eschatological Hope. Finally, Leibniz connects evil's defeat to moral and metaphysical progress within the city-metaphor (sometimes compared to a 'City of God'). Over time—and, for Leibniz, ultimately beyond this life—rational minds can advance in knowledge and charity, such that the world's narrative realizes ever greater harmony. The permission of evil is inseparable from the possibility of such growth and the achievement of the greatest overall good (Monadology, §§83, 85; Theodicy). (Leibniz, Monadology §§84–86)

Comparative Section: Leibniz and Kant on Good and Evil

Leibniz and Kant approach the problem of good and evil from distinct vantage points, yet both operate within the framework of rationalist inquiry into morality and metaphysics. Leibniz integrates ethics with metaphysics, identifying good with perfection and harmony, while evil is the privation of such perfection. Kant, by contrast, grounds morality not in metaphysical order but in the autonomy of reason: the good arises from acting out of respect for the moral law, while evil consists in subordinating that law to self-interest (Kant, Religion within the Boundaries of Mere Reason, Part One).

For Leibniz, God ensures that the created order is the best of all possible worlds, where local evils are outweighed by the greater harmony of the whole (Leibniz, Theodicy, §§5–6). Kant, however, rejects theodicies as speculative and instead emphasizes human responsibility: the root of evil lies in the propensity of the human will to prioritize inclinations over duty (Kant, Religion, Book One). While Leibniz accounts for evil within a divinely optimized cosmos, Kant situates it in the moral corruption of free agents.

Both philosophers converge in affirming that evil does not undermine the ultimate possibility of goodness. For Leibniz, evil contributes indirectly to the perfection of the whole, much like shadows enhance a painting. For Kant, moral evil can be overcome through the cultivation of virtue and adherence to the categorical imperative, demonstrating the capacity of reason to realign the will with moral law. In this way, Leibniz stresses cosmic order, whereas Kant emphasizes moral autonomy as the path toward overcoming evil.

Finally, their approaches diverge in the role of divine agency. Leibniz holds that God's wisdom guarantees the harmony of creation, ensuring that apparent defects contribute to a greater good. Kant insists instead on the self-legislation of reason, maintaining that moral worth depends upon the agent's free choice to follow duty, not upon metaphysical assurances. This distinction highlights Leibniz's reliance on metaphysical perfection versus Kant's focus on moral law and freedom as the decisive criteria for evaluating good and evil.

Simplified Summary
Leibniz sees good as perfection and harmony, and evil as a lack of perfection. God, who is perfectly wise and good, chooses to create the best possible world—one that balances simplicity of design with richness of results. In such a world, some suffering

and wrongdoing are permitted because they can be part of a greater order that produces more overall good. For people, being good means acting from wisdom and charity—seeking the good of others and the whole community. Justice is therefore 'the charity of the wise.'

We become happier as we understand the order of things more clearly and shape our choices to fit it. Evil comes from confused thinking and choosing lesser goods over higher ones, but because we act from reasons, we remain responsible and capable of moral growth. Leibniz's view ties ethics to the structure of reality: better knowledge brings deeper love and a more harmonious life. (Leibniz, Natural Law Writings; cf. 'De Justitia et Caritate')

Bibliography

Leibniz, G. W. "Discourse on Metaphysics." In *Philosophical Essays*, edited and Translated by Roger Ariew and Daniel Garber. Indianapolis: Hackett, 1989.

Leibniz, G. W. "Monadology." In *Philosophical Essays*, edited and Translated by Roger Ariew and Daniel Garber. Indianapolis: Hackett, 1989.

Leibniz, G. W. *Theodicy: Essays on the Goodness of God, the Freedom of Man and the Origin of

Evil*. Translated by E. M. Huggard. La Salle, IL: Open Court, 1985 (orig. 1710).

Leibniz, G. W. "Meditation on the Common Concept of Justice," "Felicity," and selections from *Codex Iuris Gentium*. In *Philosophical Essays*, edited by Roger Ariew and Daniel Garber. Indianapolis: Hackett, 1989.

Allison, Henry E. *Leibniz: Discourse on Metaphysics and Related Writings*. New Haven: Yale University Press, 1998.

Adams, Robert Merrihew. *Leibniz: Determinist, Theist, Idealist*. New York: Oxford University Press, 1994.

Jolley, Nicholas, ed. *The Cambridge Companion to Leibniz*. Cambridge: Cambridge University Press, 1995.

Garber, Daniel. *Leibniz: Body, Substance, Monad*. Oxford: Oxford University Press, 2009.

Kant, Immanuel. Religion within the Boundaries of Mere Reason. Translated by Allen Wood and George di Giovanni. Cambridge: Cambridge University Press, 1998.

Kant, Immanuel. Critique of Practical Reason. Translated by Mary Gregor. Cambridge: Cambridge University Press, 1997.

Suggested Reading

Antognazza, Maria Rosa. *Leibniz: An Intellectual Biography*. Cambridge: Cambridge University Press, 2009.

Jorgensen, Larry M., and Samuel Newlands, eds. *Leibniz's Theodicy: A Critical Guide*. Cambridge: Cambridge University Press, 2014.

Murray, Michael J. *Leibniz on the Problem of Evil*. Oxford: Oxford University Press, 2008.

Antognazza, Maria Rosa, ed. *The Oxford Handbook of Leibniz*. Oxford: Oxford University Press, 2018.

Look, Brandon C., ed. *The Bloomsbury Companion to Leibniz*. London: Bloomsbury Academic, 2017.

Leibniz, G. W. *New Essays on Human Understanding*. Translated and edited by Peter Remnant and Jonathan Bennett. Cambridge: Cambridge University Press, 1996.

Leibniz, G. W. *Political Writings*. Edited by Patrick Riley. 2nd ed. Cambridge: Cambridge University Press, 1988.

Rutherford, Donald. *Leibniz and the Rational Order of Nature*. Cambridge: Cambridge University Press, 1995.

Leibniz, G. W. *Philosophical Essays*. Translated by Roger Ariew and Daniel Garber. Hackett, 1989.

Leibniz, G. W. *Discourse on Metaphysics and Other Essays*. Translated by Daniel Garber and Roger Ariew. Hackett, 1991.

Leibniz, G. W. *Theodicy: Essays on the Goodness of God, the Freedom of Man and the Origin of Evil*. Translated by E. M. Huggard. Open Court, 1985.

Kant, Immanuel. *Religion within the Boundaries of Mere Reason*. Translated by Allen Wood and George di Giovanni. Cambridge University Press, 1998.

Kant, Immanuel. "On the Miscarriage of All Philosophical Trials in Theodicy." In *Religion and Rational Theology*, edited and Translated by Allen W. Wood and George di Giovanni, Cambridge University Press, 1996.

Stanford Encyclopedia of Philosophy. "Gottfried Wilhelm Leibniz," and "Leibniz's Ethics," and "Kant's Moral Philosophy." (peer-reviewed, regularly updated).

Three Modern Questions and Likely Responses

1) How would Leibniz address modern natural disasters (earthquakes, pandemics) that cause immense suffering?

Within his framework, these belong to *physical evil* (pain/suffering). He holds that God permits—does not will—such evils within the **best overall plan**, where local ills can be conditions for greater goods and a richer, law-governed order. This follows his triad of evils and the theodicean claim that even the best possible world can contain some evil, while remaining optimal in the whole. (Leibniz, *Theodicy* T §21; *Discourse on Metaphysics* §6.)

2) What would he say to today's moral relativism and cultural diversity in ethics?

Leibniz roots morality in *eternal truths* accessible to reason, not in shifting custom; justice is "the charity of the wise," i.e., rational benevolence ordered by wisdom. He can acknowledge cultural variation in laws/practices while denying that such variation undermines universal principles aimed at perfection and the common good. (SEP, "Leibniz's Ethics"; Riley, *Leibniz' Universal Jurisprudence*.)

3) Isn't "the best of all possible worlds" naïve in light of wars, genocides, and technological risks? Leibniz's optimism concerns the *total history* optimized by divine wisdom: God selects the world that is **simplest in laws and richest in phenomena**, where permitting certain evils is tied to realizing the greatest overall harmony. That does not excuse wrongdoing; rather, rational agents are obligated to act wisely and charitably to reduce suffering and increase perfection. (Leibniz, *Discourse* §6; SEP, "Leibniz's Modal Metaphysics"; SEP, "Leibniz's Ethics".)

Baruch Spinoza

Biography

Spinoza's personal life was marked by modesty and independence. After his excommunication, he declined offers of prestigious academic positions, such as a chair at Heidelberg, to preserve his intellectual freedom. He supported himself through grinding optical lenses, gaining a reputation for technical skill, while writing treatises that would later secure his status among the great philosophers of the Enlightenment. His correspondence with leading figures of the era, including Henry Oldenburg and Leibniz, reveals both his careful reasoning and the controversies surrounding his ideas. (Nadler 1999, ch. 10–12.)

Although denounced as an 'atheist' by many contemporaries, Spinoza's identification of God with Nature was not a rejection of divinity but a redefinition of it. He conceived God as an infinite substance expressing itself through infinite attributes, of which thought and extension are known to us. This theological naturalism reshaped metaphysics, inspiring admiration and hostility alike. His Ethics was placed on the Index of Prohibited Books, yet its impact on philosophy, theology, and science has endured. (E1p14; E1app; Melamed 2013, ch. 1.)

Baruch (Benedict) Spinoza (1632–1677) was a Dutch philosopher of Sephardic Jewish origin and one of the major rationalists of the seventeenth century. Born in Amsterdam and educated in the Jewish community, he was excommunicated in 1656 for heterodox views and thereafter lived modestly as a lens grinder while developing a systematic philosophy. His magnum opus, the Ethics—published posthumously in 1677—presents a rigorous metaphysics, epistemology, and moral psychology in geometric form. He also wrote The Theological-Political Treatise (published anonymously in 1670), defending freedom of thought and the subordination of theology to philosophy, and the unfinished Political Treatise. Spinoza's radical monism (Deus sive Natura: God or Nature) identifies one infinite substance of which all things are modes, a view that profoundly influenced the Enlightenment. (E1app; TTP ch.16; PT ch.1.)

Summary of Views on Good and Evil

For Spinoza, because reality is a single necessary order—God or Nature—nothing is intrinsically good or evil. Good and evil are ways we describe how things affect our power of acting and our striving to persevere (conatus). "By good I understand what we certainly know is useful to us," and by evil what hinders our power (E4def1; E4pref). The more adequate our ideas, the more we act from reason and attain blessedness (beatitudo), culminating in the intellectual love of God (amor Dei intellectualis). True freedom is rational self-determination within necessity. (E3p6–p9; E4p18; E5p32–p36.)

Spinoza on Good

Relative, Not Absolute. Good is not an intrinsic property of things but expresses their relation to our nature—what increases our power of acting or accords with our rational constitution. Judgments of good vary with perspective. (E4pref; E4def1.)

Conatus and Human Flourishing. Each thing strives to persevere in its being (conatus). For humans, genuine goods are those that reliably empower this striving under the guidance of reason, as opposed to merely apparent goods tied to passive affects. (E3p6–p9; E4p18–p19.)

The Role of Reason and the Common Good.
Reason reveals that cooperative life—justice,

fairness, friendship—best secures our advantage, so the good extends to the common good. (E4p18; E4p35–p37.)

Blessedness and Intellectual Love of God. The highest good is eternal and intellectual: adequate knowledge leading to the intellectual love of God, a joy that cannot be diminished by fortune. (E5p32–p36.)

Knowledge and Freedom. To act from adequate ideas is to act from one's essence understood through reason; knowledge and virtue coincide. (E4p24; E5p2.)

Spinoza on Evil

Privation and Relativity. Evil is not an absolute feature of reality but names what diminishes our power or conflicts with our nature. Poison is 'evil' for humans, though it may be 'good' for other organisms. (E4pref; E4def2.)

Passions and Bondage. Bondage to the passions—emotions arising from inadequate ideas—reduces our activity and renders us dependent on external causes. (E3p1–p3; E4pref.)

Ignorance as Source of Evil. Since all things follow necessarily from the divine nature, ignorance and inadequate perception make us call things 'evil.'

God neither wills nor permits evil; the label reflects our standpoint. (E1app; E4pref.)

Discord and Social Harm. Strife, injustice, and tyranny are evils because they undermine the cooperative conditions reason prescribes for flourishing. (TTP ch.16; ch.20.)

Overcoming Evil. The remedy is intellectual: cultivating adequate ideas, transforming passive affects into active ones, and living according to reason—culminating in blessedness, which dissolves the perspective of evil. (E5p3–p42.)

Comparative: Spinoza and Leibniz on Good and Evil

Both Spinoza and Leibniz are rationalists, but they diverge sharply on good, evil, and freedom. For Spinoza, good and evil are relative to our conatus and reflect epistemic position; evil dissolves with adequate knowledge. For Leibniz, goods and evils have an objective standing within the divine choice of the best possible world, with a tripartite taxonomy—metaphysical (privation), physical (suffering), and moral (sin). (Leibniz, Theodicy §20, §21; cf. Youpa 2004.) Spinoza's freedom is acting from the necessity of one's nature understood through reason; Leibnizian freedom is rational inclination compatible with divine preordination. Both culminate in an intellectual joy—Spinoza's amor Dei intellectualis and Leibniz's participation in divine wisdom—but they disagree on God's relation to evil: Spinoza denies divine willing or permitting of evil (since 'evil' is perspectival), whereas Leibniz holds that God permits evils for greater overall good in the optimal design. (E1app; E5p32–p36; Theodicy §§193–204.)

Simplified Summary

Spinoza says nothing is absolutely good or evil. We call things good when they help us live and grow, and evil when they hold us back. The best life is using reason to understand nature and ourselves, leading to a steady joy and the 'intellectual love of God.' Evil comes from ignorance and harmful passions, but knowledge and self-control can overcome it. Leibniz disagrees: he treats evil as real (though permitted by God) in a world designed for the greatest overall good.

Notes on Sources

Inline references follow a compact scheme for Spinoza's Ethics: (E<book><locus>), e.g., (E4def1), (E1app), (E3p6–p9), (E5p32–p36). The Theological-Political Treatise is cited as (TTP ch.N) and the Political Treatise as (PT ch.N). Unless otherwise stated, translations are from Edwin Curley's editions. Secondary literature is included for context and further reading.

Bibliography

Spinoza, Benedict de. Ethics. In The Collected Works of Spinoza, Volume I, edited and translated by Edwin Curley. Princeton, NJ: Princeton University Press, 1985.

Spinoza, Benedict de. Political Treatise. In The Collected Works of Spinoza, Volume II, edited and translated by Edwin Curley. Princeton, NJ: Princeton University Press, 2016.

Spinoza, Benedict de. Theological-Political Treatise. Edited by Jonathan Israel. Translated by Michael Silverthorne and Jonathan Israel. Cambridge: Cambridge University Press, 2007.

Leibniz, G. W. Theodicy. Translated by E. M. Huggard. La Salle, IL: Open Court, 1985.

Nadler, Steven. Spinoza: A Life. Cambridge: Cambridge University Press, 1999.

Garrett, Don. Meaning in Spinoza's Method. Cambridge: Cambridge University Press, 2003.

Melamed, Yitzhak Y. Spinoza's Metaphysics: Substance and Thought. Oxford: Oxford University Press, 2013.

Youpa, Andrew. "Leibniz' Ethics." In The Stanford Encyclopedia of Philosophy (Summer 2014 Edition), ed. Edward N. Zalta.

Steinberg, Justin. "Spinoza's Political Philosophy." In The Stanford Encyclopedia of Philosophy (Spring 2023 Edition), ed. Edward N. Zalta.

Simplified Summary Addendum

Spinoza believed that nothing in nature is absolutely good or bad. Things are called good when they help us live, grow, and use our reason; they are called evil when they harm us or weaken us. For him, the best life is one guided by reason, which allows us to find steady happiness and a deep love of God understood as Nature itself. He thought that many problems come from ignorance and strong emotions like fear or anger, but knowledge and self-control can free us. Compared to Leibniz, who said evil is a real part of God's plan for the best possible world, Spinoza taught that evil is only a matter of our limited viewpoint and disappears when we understand reality clearly.

Jean-Jacques Rousseau on Good and Evil

Biography

Jean-Jacques Rousseau (1712–1778) was a
Genevan-born philosopher, writer, and composer
whose works shaped Enlightenment thought, the
French Revolution, and modern political
philosophy. After early success with the First
Discourse—*Discourse on the Sciences and Arts*
(1750)—he developed his moral psychology and
political theory in the Second Discourse—
*Discourse on the Origin and Foundations of
Inequality Among Men* (1755)—and in *The
Social Contract* (1762). He also wrote *Émile*
(1762), a work on education and human
development. These later books were condemned
(Paris and Geneva, 1762), and Rousseau spent years
in exile before returning to France; he died at
Ermenonville in 1778. (SEP, "Rousseau"; *Social
Contract* I.1; *Émile*, Bloom trans.; historical
timeline in SEP/IEP).

Born in Geneva to a watchmaker father and losing
his mother shortly after birth, Rousseau's early years
were marked by intermittent schooling, an

apprenticeship to an engraver, and a restless independence that culminated in his flight from Geneva in 1728. In Savoy he came under the protection of Françoise-Louise de Warens ("Maman"), whose patronage shaped his education and religious turns; he briefly converted to Catholicism before later reconverting to Genevan Protestantism in 1754. During these formative years, he pursued music theory and composition, drafted opera and theoretical writings on notation, and developed a suspicion of courtly polish and theatrical display that would reappear in his mature critiques of luxury and spectacle.

By the 1740s–50s Rousseau was moving among the Paris philosophes, contributing notable articles on music to Diderot's *Encyclopédie* and winning fame with the prize essay now called the First Discourse (1750). His later works—*Discourse on Inequality* (1755), *Émile* and *The Social Contract* (both 1762)—provoked official condemnation in Geneva and Paris, forcing a peripatetic exile (Neuchâtel/Môtiers, then England at David Hume's invitation in 1766) before a quiet return to France. In his final decade, he supported himself by copying music and composed reflective autobiographical works—*Confessions* and *Reveries of the Solitary Walker*. He died in 1778 at Ermenonville; his remains were transferred to the

Panthéon in 1794, emblematic of his enduring civic and intellectual legacy.

Summary of Views on Good and Evil

Rousseau holds that humans are by nature good but are corrupted by social development. In the state of nature, people are guided by natural self-love (*amour de soi*) and compassion (*pitié*). Evil arises with the emergence of private property, comparative self-love (*amour-propre*), and the inequalities and dependencies of civilization. Goodness is preserved by cultivating natural sentiments and, at the political level, by establishing institutions ordered to the common good—the general will—rather than to private interests. (Second Discourse, Part I–II; *Social Contract* I.6, II.3–4, IV.1; SEP "Rousseau").

Rousseau on Good

Natural Goodness. Humans are naturally inclined to self-preservation (*amour de soi*) and to compassion (*pitié*), which restrains cruelty and makes us recoil at the suffering of others. These pre-rational sentiments ground a baseline goodness prior to social corruption. (Second Discourse, Part I; SEP "Rousseau").

The Role of Compassion. Against Hobbesian pessimism, Rousseau emphasizes an innate capacity for empathy—the immediate, affective response to others' pain—rather than abstract moral reasoning as the first source of moral concern. (Second Discourse, Part I; SEP "Rousseau").

Education and the Cultivation of Good. In *Émile*, proper education shields the child from premature social influences so that natural autonomy and compassion can mature without being deformed by vanity and competition. (Émile, Book I–II; Bloom trans.).

Freedom and the General Will. Political right is realized when each person, joining with all, obeys laws he has prescribed together with others—"each of us puts his person and all his power in common under the supreme direction of the general will." This reconciles individual freedom with the common good. (*Social Contract* I.6; IV.1.)

Authenticity and Simplicity. Rousseau criticizes the artificiality of status-seeking and luxury; the good life favors sincerity, simplicity, and closeness to natural sentiments. (First Discourse).

Rousseau on Evil
Corruption through Society. "Man is born free, and everywhere he is in chains": evil is a product of

social arrangements that distort natural goodness. Dependence, rivalry, and domination proliferate as societies develop. (*Social Contract* I.1; Second Discourse, Part II.)

Private Property and Inequality. Moral evil begins when property, wealth, and rank introduce comparisons and dependence—"the first man who, having enclosed a piece of ground, said 'This is mine' … was the true founder of civil society." (Second Discourse, Part II.)

Amour-Propre and Social Vice. In society, natural self-love is transformed into comparative self-love (*amour-propre*), which, when unchecked, enslaves us to opinion and breeds jealousy, ambition, and domination; in a well-ordered polity, *amour-propre* can be redirected toward civic virtue. (Émile IV; SEP "Rousseau".)

Despotism and the Loss of Freedom. When governments act for private interest rather than the general will, the body politic degenerates; the sovereign is suppressed, and citizens lose freedom. (*Social Contract* III.10; IV.1.)

Rousseau argues that luxury and the pursuit of prestige corrupt civic character by redirecting attention from virtue to appearance. Because esteem becomes competitive, *amour-propre* turns positional and breeds dependence on others' opinions, undermining freedom and the common good. (First Discourse; Social Contract I.8–I.10).

Rousseau, Jean-Jacques. *The Social Contract and Other Later Political Writings*. Edited by Victor Gourevitch. Cambridge: Cambridge University Press, 1997.

Rousseau, Jean-Jacques. *The Discourses and Other Early Political Writings*. Edited by Victor Gourevitch. Cambridge: Cambridge University Press, 1997.

Rousseau, Jean-Jacques. *Émile, or On Education*. Translated by Allan Bloom. New York: Basic Books, 1979.

Dent, N. J. H. *A Rousseau Dictionary*. Oxford: Blackwell, 1992.

Starobinski, Jean. *Jean-Jacques Rousseau: Transparency and Obstruction*. Translated by Arthur Goldhammer. Chicago: University of Chicago Press, 1988.

Cranston, Maurice. *Jean-Jacques: The Early Life and Work of Jean-Jacques Rousseau, 1712–1754*. Chicago: University of Chicago Press, 1982.

Kelly, Christopher. *Rousseau as Author: Consecrating One's Life to the Truth*. Chicago: University of Chicago Press, 2003.

Rousseau, Jean-Jacques. *The Confessions*. Translated by Angela Scholar. Oxford: Oxford University Press, 2000.

Rousseau, Jean-Jacques. *Reveries of the Solitary Walker*. Translated by Peter France. Oxford: Oxford University Press, 2004.

Neuhouser, Frederick. *Rousseau's Theodicy of Self-Love: Evil, Rationality, and the Drive for Recognition*. Oxford: Oxford University Press, 2008.

Riley, Patrick, ed. *The Cambridge Companion to Rousseau*. Cambridge: Cambridge University Press, 2001.

Scott, John T., ed. *Rousseau and the Social Contract*. London/New York: Routledge, 2006.

Delaney, James. "Jean-Jacques Rousseau." *The Stanford Encyclopedia of Philosophy* (latest substantive revision).

Simplified Summary

Jean-Jacques Rousseau (1712–1778) believed that humans are naturally good, guided by basic self-love and compassion. He thought that society, with its inequality and obsession with reputation, often corrupts this goodness. Rousseau argued that true freedom means following laws that we create for ourselves together, through what he called the 'general will.'

For Rousseau, education should protect children's natural goodness and guide them gradually toward moral responsibility. He warned that wealth, luxury, and the desire to impress others lead to envy, pride, and unhappiness. Despite facing exile for his controversial ideas, his works like *The Social Contract* and *Émile* remain influential in debates on freedom, justice, and education.

Bibliography

Rousseau, Jean-Jacques. *The Social Contract and Other Later Political Writings*. Edited and translated by Victor Gourevitch. Cambridge: Cambridge University Press, 1997.

Rousseau, Jean-Jacques. *The Discourses and Other Early Political Writings*. Edited and translated by Victor Gourevitch. Cambridge: Cambridge University Press, 1997.

Rousseau, Jean-Jacques. *Émile: Or On Education*. Translated by Allan Bloom. New York: Basic Books, 1979.

Dent, N. J. H. *A Rousseau Dictionary*. Oxford: Blackwell, 1992.

Starobinski, Jean. *Jean-Jacques Rousseau: Transparency and Obstruction*. Translated by Arthur Goldhammer. Chicago: University of Chicago Press, 1988.

Cranston, Maurice. *Jean-Jacques: The Early Life and Work of Jean-Jacques Rousseau, 1712–1754*. Chicago: University of Chicago Press, 1982.

Kelly, Christopher. *Rousseau as Author: Consecrating One's Life to the Truth*. Chicago: University of Chicago Press, 2003.

Neuhouser, Frederick. *Rousseau's Theodicy of Self-Love: Evil, Rationality, and the Drive for Recognition*. Oxford: Oxford University Press, 2008.

Riley, Patrick. *The General Will before Rousseau: The Transformation of the Divine into the Civic*. Princeton: Princeton University Press, 1986.

Cohen, Joshua. *Rousseau: A Free Community of Equals*. Oxford: Oxford University Press, 2010.

Bertram, Christopher. "Jean Jacques Rousseau." In *The Stanford Encyclopedia of Philosophy* (Fall 2023 Edition), Edward N. Zalta and Uri Nodelman (eds.). First published September 27, 2010; substantive revision April 21, 2023.

Delaney, James J. "Jean-Jacques Rousseau (1712–1778)." *Internet Encyclopedia of Philosophy*, 2005 .

David Hume

Biography

David Hume (1711–1776) was a Scottish philosopher, historian, and essayist whose work reshaped modern moral psychology and ethics. Educated at the University of Edinburgh, Hume developed an empiricist program that grounded knowledge and morality in experience. His major philosophical writings include the three-volume *Treatise of Human Nature* (1739–1740), the later and more accessible *Enquiry concerning Human Understanding* (1748), and the *Enquiry concerning the Principles of Morals* (1751). Alongside these works, Hume published essays on politics, aesthetics, and religion, and composed the posthumously published *Dialogues concerning Natural Religion*. His ethical philosophy—rooted in sentiment, sympathy, and social convention—stands in deliberate contrast to the rationalist systems of the seventeenth and eighteenth centuries.

After early study at the University of Edinburgh, Hume briefly tried commerce in Bristol (1734), found it unsuitable, and soon departed for France, living frugally and working first at Reims and then at La Flèche. There, between 1734–1737, he drafted the *Treatise of Human Nature* before returning to London to publish it (1739–1740).

Hume's public career included service as Librarian to the Faculty of Advocates (1752)—access that enabled his bestselling six-volume *History of England* (1754–1762)—followed by diplomatic and civil posts as Secretary to the British Embassy in Paris (1763–1766) and Under-Secretary of State, Northern Department (1767–1768). In his brief autobiography "My Own Life" (1777), he judged the *Enquiry concerning the Principles of Morals* his best work. He died in Edinburgh in 1776.

Summary of Views on Good and Evil

Hume argues that moral distinctions are derived not from reason alone but from sentiment: we approve or disapprove of traits and actions because of how they feel from a common human point of view. Reason, in his picture, discovers facts and relations, but it is sentiment—shaped by sympathy and a shared standpoint—that confers moral value. 'Reason is, and ought only to be the slave of the passions,' Hume famously writes; it can direct means to ends but does not supply ends by itself (Treatise 2.3.3.4). Hence, ideas of good and evil track patterns of approbation and blame that emerge when we adopt the 'common point of view' and consider the utility and agreeableness of qualities to ourselves and others (EPM Sec. V; Sec. IX).

Hume on Good

Sentiment and the Common Point of View. Hume holds that moral evaluation depends on how a trait affects human welfare when assessed from a general perspective. We correct for personal bias by adopting a 'common point of view,' allowing sympathy to extend our concern beyond our private circle. What we call good are traits that, viewed generally, prove useful or agreeable to self or others—benevolence, gratitude, temperance, prudence, wit—because such traits promote human flourishing (Treatise 3.1.2; EPM Sec. V, Sec. IX).

Natural and Artificial Virtues. Hume distinguishes 'natural' virtues (e.g., benevolence, generosity) from 'artificial' virtues (e.g., justice, fidelity to promises). Natural virtues spring directly from human affections and are broadly admired across contexts; artificial virtues arise from social conventions that structure cooperation in conditions of limited generosity and scarce resources. The goodness of justice does not lie in an intrinsic property but in its role within a convention that secures mutual advantage (Treatise 3.2.1; EPM Sec. III–IV).

Utility and Agreeableness as Sources of Moral Approbation. In the *Enquiry concerning the

Principles of Morals*, Hume argues that the principal grounds of moral approval are utility (usefulness) and agreeableness. We approve qualities like industry and honesty because they contribute to social prosperity; we also approve charms like good humor because they make social life agreeable. This does not reduce morality to crude self-interest: sympathy enables us to take pleasure in the happiness of others as if it were our own (EPM Sec. V).

Reason's Role. Reason remains indispensable, but as an auxiliary: it informs us of facts, consequences, and causal connections, thus guiding the application of our sentiments. Hume's famous 'is–ought' remark cautions against illicitly inferring obligations from bare descriptions; the transition to 'ought' requires reference to sentiments and ends that agents actually endorse (Treatise 3.1.1).

Character and Moral Education. For Hume, good is primarily a quality of character rather than of isolated actions. Habits cultivate stable dispositions that evoke approval from the common point of view. Education and institutions can refine our sentiments, widening sympathy and making the public interest a source of individual satisfaction (EPM Sec. IX).

Hume on Evil

Vice as Disapproved Character. Evil, in Hume's framework, is not a metaphysical force or violation of eternal forms; it is the class of traits and actions that elicit stable disapproval from the common point of view—cruelty, treachery, ingratitude, injustice. We condemn these because they predictably undermine human well-being and disrupt social life (Treatise 3.1.2; EPM Sec. IX).

Passions, Partiality, and Corruption. Hume's psychology highlights sources of moral failure: violent passions, narrow partiality, and superstition can overpower calm reflection and sympathy. When partiality dominates, we overvalue our own interests and factions; when superstition prevails, we mistake imagined obligations for genuine virtues (EPM Sec. IX; Dialogues Pt. X–XI).

Justice, Convention, and the Conditions of Vice. Because justice is an artificial virtue sustained by convention, vice flourishes when the conventions that sustain property, promise-keeping, and allegiance are undermined by scarcity, faction, or predation. Hume explains why strict rules of justice are suspended in extreme necessity (shipwreck, famine), revealing that the morality of justice depends on background conditions that make cooperation possible (Treatise 3.2.2; EPM Sec. III).

The Is–Ought Gap and Fanaticism. Hume warns that moralists who treat descriptive claims as if they entailed obligations court fanaticism. Projecting one's preferences as absolute 'oughts' licenses persecution and cruelty. By insisting that obligation arises within human sentiment and convention, Hume seeks to curb zeal and promote humane moderation (Treatise 3.1.1; EPM Sec. IX).

Religion and the Problem of Evil. In the *Dialogues*, Hume challenges theodicies that attempt to reconcile omnipotence and perfect goodness with pervasive suffering. Without committing to atheism, he argues that the empirical evidence underdetermines the claim of a providential moral order. Whatever our metaphysics, moral evaluation must remain anchored in human sentiments and the harms and benefits we actually observe (Dialogues Pt. X–XI).

Comparative Section: Hume and Rousseau on Good and Evil

Historical Connection. Hume and Rousseau were near contemporaries who briefly allied before falling out. In 1766, Hume invited the exiled Rousseau to Britain and helped secure support for him, but their relationship quickly soured amid mutual suspicions. The exchange culminated in Hume's public pamphlet, *A Concise and Genuine Account of the

Dispute between Mr. Hume and Mr. Rousseau*
(1766), and in their published correspondence
(Leigh, *The Rousseau–Hume Correspondence*).
The episode reflects their temperamental and
philosophical differences.

Philosophical Contrast. Rousseau locates evil in
social corruption—especially the rise of property,
inequality, and amour-propre—while identifying the
good with natural compassion, authenticity, and a
political order that embodies the general will
(Rousseau, *Discourse on Inequality*, Pt. II;
Social Contract I.6). Hume, by contrast, explains
good and evil through sentiment, sympathy, and
convention. For him, virtues are traits that win stable
approval from the common point of view because
they are useful or agreeable; vices predictably harm
social life (EPM Sec. V, Sec. IX). Both reject
rationalist metaphysics in morals, but Rousseau
casts society as the principal corrupter, whereas
Hume emphasizes how sentiments can be educated
to sustain cooperative conventions and mitigate
partiality.

Simplified Summary
Hume says morality comes from feeling, not from
pure reason. We call traits good when, from a shared
human standpoint, they prove useful or agreeable to
ourselves and others; we call traits evil when they

predictably harm people and disrupt social life. Benevolence is naturally good; justice is an 'artificial' virtue created by social rules that help us cooperate. Hume warns against deriving moral rules from bare facts and argues that sympathy and education can widen our concern for others. Compared with Rousseau—who sees society as the main source of corruption—Hume believes our sentiments, properly trained, make social cooperation and stable morality possible.

Bibliography

Hume, David. *A Treatise of Human Nature*. Edited by L. A. Selby-Bigge, revised by P. H. Nidditch. Oxford: Clarendon Press, 1978 (orig. 1739–40).

Hume, David. *An Enquiry concerning the Principles of Morals*. Edited by Tom L. Beauchamp. Oxford: Oxford University Press, 1998 (orig. 1751).

Hume, David. *An Enquiry concerning Human Understanding*. Edited by Tom L. Beauchamp. Oxford: Oxford University Press, 2000 (orig. 1748).

Hume, David. *Dialogues concerning Natural Religion*. Edited by J. C. A. Gaskin. Oxford: Oxford University Press, 1993.

Hume, David. *A Concise and Genuine Account of the Dispute between Mr. Hume and Mr. Rousseau*. London, 1766.

Leigh, R. A., ed. *The Rousseau–Hume Correspondence*. Manchester: Manchester University Press, 1963.

Baier, Annette. *A Progress of Sentiments: Reflections on Hume's Treatise of Human Nature*. Cambridge, MA: Harvard University Press, 1991.

Cohon, Rachel. *Hume's Morality: Feeling and Fabrication*. Oxford: Oxford University Press, 2008.

Norton, David Fate, and Jacqueline Taylor, eds. *The Cambridge Companion to Hume*, 2nd ed. Cambridge: Cambridge University Press, 2009.

Hume, David. "My Own Life." In *The Life of David Hume, Esq. Written by Himself*. London: W. Strahan and T. Cadell, 1777.

Hume, David. *The History of England*. 6 vols. London, 1754–1762.

Arthur Schopenhauer

Biography

Arthur Schopenhauer (1788–1860) was a German philosopher whose system—best known from *The World as Will and Representation* (1818/1844)—unified metaphysics, aesthetics, and ethics around the claim that the inner essence of reality is will. Born in Danzig (Gdańsk) and educated in Göttingen and Berlin, he wrote a dissertation on the fourfold root of the principle of sufficient reason before producing his magnum opus. His major ethical writings include *On the Basis of Morality* (1840) and the prize essay *On the Freedom of the Will* (1839), later gathered with additional essays in *Parerga and Paralipomena* (1851). Initially neglected, his work gained wide influence late in his life and after his death, shaping debates in philosophy, psychology, and literature.

Schopenhauer was born on February 22, 1788, to the merchant Heinrich Floris Schopenhauer and the novelist Johanna Schopenhauer in the then-Free City of Danzig. After Prussia annexed Danzig (1793), the family relocated to Hamburg. As a youth, he was apprenticed in commerce and traveled through

France and England (1803–1804), but following his father's death in 1805, he pursued formal studies. In 1809, he enrolled at the University of Göttingen, beginning in medicine and quickly shifting to philosophy under the influence of G. E. Schulze's rigorous post-Kantian skepticism. He attended lectures in Berlin in 1811–1813, yet found the prevailing idealism uncongenial, completing instead at Jena his doctoral dissertation On the Fourfold Root of the Principle of Sufficient Reason (1813). (Cartwright 2010, 112–18, chs. 1–4; Janaway 2002, 55–60.)

From 1814, he spent time in Weimar, conversing with Goethe and composing On Vision and Colors (1816), a study that engages with Goethe's theory of color while advancing Schopenhauer's own account of perception. The first edition of The World as Will and Representation appeared in 1818, and he became a privatdozent in Berlin (1820), ill-fatedly scheduling his lectures opposite Hegel's— attendance was scant, and he soon withdrew from academic life. During the 1831 cholera epidemic, he left Berlin, settling by 1833 in Frankfurt am Main, where he lived quietly for the rest of his life. His essay On the Freedom of the Will won the prize of the Royal Norwegian Society of Sciences in 1839; its companion, On the Basis of Morality, was rejected by the Royal Danish Society in 1840 but published with the former in 1841. The two-volume Parerga and Paralipomena (1851) finally brought broad recognition and a devoted readership. He died in Frankfurt on September 21, 1860. (Cartwright 2010, 112–18, chs. 5–9; Janaway 1999, 78–84.)

Summary of Views on Good and Evil

Schopenhauer grounds ethics in a metaphysics of will and a moral psychology centered on compassion (*Mitleid*). At the metaphysical level, the world we know in experience is representation, while the thing-in-itself is will—a blind, striving force that expresses itself through all of nature and in us as desire. Because willing is endless and satisfaction fleeting, existence is pervaded by suffering. From this diagnosis flow two complementary ethical paths. First, the ordinary moral life aims to reduce harm and relieve suffering through justice and benevolence, whose sole genuine motive is compassion. Second, a more radical ideal—the saint's denial of the will—seeks deliverance from suffering by loosening the grip of desire through ascetic discipline and clear insight into the nature of the world. In both paths, 'good' is indexed to the lessening or overcoming of suffering;

'evil' is bound up with egoism, cruelty, and the affirmation of will at others' expense (WWR I, Book IV; *On the Basis of Morality*; *Parerga and Paralipomena*).

Schopenhauer on Good

Compassion as the Sole Moral Motive.
In *On the Basis of Morality*, Schopenhauer argues that only compassion explains genuine moral worth. Acts moved merely by prudence, reputation, religious reward, or abstract principle lack moral value; what makes an action good is that the agent's own interest is overruled by direct participation in another's suffering. Compassion reveals the metaphysical unity behind the phenomenal multiplicity—our insight that 'the inner nature in you and me is one and the same.' Hence, benevolence and justice are good because they spring from this shared feeling for the other (*On the Basis of Morality*, Preface and Part I).

Justice (Non-Injury) and Loving-Kindness (Beneficence).
Schopenhauer distinguishes 'negative' virtue (justice) from 'positive' virtue (loving-kindness). Justice refrains from harming others; beneficence

actively relieves their suffering. The hierarchy matters: the first duty is to cause no harm, then to help where we can. In social life, the rules of justice—property, fidelity, honesty—translate compassion into stable norms that protect the vulnerable (*On the Basis of Morality*, Part II).

Aesthetics and the Quieting of the Will.
Although not a moral achievement in itself, aesthetic contemplation provides a foretaste of the good by suspending willing. In experiencing the beautiful or the sublime, we become 'pure subject of knowing,' temporarily liberated from restless desire. This respite clarifies why the good life involves diminishing the tyranny of the will: peace comes in proportion to the stilling of craving (WWR I, Book III).

Asceticism and the Denial of the Will.
The higher ethical ideal, presented in WWR I and II, is the saint's renunciation of egoistic striving—chastity, poverty, humility, and universal benevolence. Such practices are not arbitrary rules but expressions of insight into the essence of things: to will less is to suffer less. Schopenhauer reads the ethical kernels of Christianity, as well as elements of Indian traditions, as converging on this denial of the will (WWR I, Book IV; *Parerga and Paralipomena*, "On Ethics").

Freedom, Character, and Responsibility.
In *On the Freedom of the Will*, Schopenhauer distinguishes empirical character (governed by causal necessity) from intelligible character (the timeless root of who we are). We are not 'free' in the everyday sense of indifferent choice, yet we are responsible insofar as our deeds express our intelligible character. Moral improvement is therefore a transformation in the ground of willing—rare, but possible—and good actions manifest a will in which compassion predominates over egoism (*On the Freedom of the Will*; WWR I, Book IV).

Schopenhauer on Evil

Egoism as the Root of Vice.
If compassion is the sole moral motive, egoism is the root of evil. The egoist recognizes only his own will as important, treating others as mere means. Cruelty is the extreme of egoism: the positive enjoyment of another's suffering. Both deny the unity disclosed in compassion and intensify the world's suffering (*On the Basis of Morality*, Part II; *Parerga and Paralipomena*, "On the Suffering of the World").

Affirmation of the Will.

Evil is bound up with the affirmation of life-will: the drive to live, consume, dominate, and reproduce without limit. Because willing is endless, every affirmation multiplies new lacks and new pains. Schopenhauer's pessimism is ethical as well as metaphysical: the more the will asserts itself, the more pervasive the frustration and conflict—hence the ubiquity of harm in human affairs (WWR I, Book IV).

Suffering as the World's Baseline.

Schopenhauer rejects the optimism that normalizes happiness and treats suffering as an anomaly. Pain, want, boredom, and death are structural features of a world expressed as will. To call an arrangement 'evil' is to mark the amplification of these evils by egoism and malice; to call institutions or acts 'good' is to the extent that they reduce preventable suffering (*Parerga and Paralipomena*, "On the Suffering of the World").

Religion, Morality, and Misused Motives.

Schopenhauer criticizes moralities that ground duty in reward, punishment, or abstract rational law. Such extrinsic motives, he argues, cannot produce genuine virtue; at best, they discipline behavior, at worst, they sanctify cruelty in the name of principle. Where religion cultivates compassion and ascetic self-restraint, it allies with the good; where it fuels persecution or glorifies mortification for its own sake, it allies with evil (WWR I, Book IV; *Parerga and Paralipomena*, "On Ethics").

Freedom, Guilt, and Evil Will.
While empirical actions are necessitated by motives and character, the intelligible character may be faulted or praised. Thus, Schopenhauer can say that evil is not a metaphysical substance but the expression of a will set against the suffering of others. Guilt attaches not to isolated outcomes but to the quality of will they manifest—above all, whether egoism or compassion rules (*On the Freedom of the Will*).

Simplified Summary

Schopenhauer believes the world's inner nature is will: a blind striving that makes life restless and full of suffering. Good actions come from compassion— direct concern for others—which becomes justice (not harming) and kindness (helping). Beauty gives us a brief rest from desire, and the highest ideal is to weaken the will's grip through humility and restraint. Evil grows from egoism and cruelty, the refusal to see ourselves in others. We are not free in every choice, but we are responsible because our deeds express our deeper character. The more compassion rules our will, the less we add to the world's suffering.

Bibliography

Schopenhauer, Arthur. *The World as Will and Representation*, Vols. I–II. Translated by E. F. J. Payne. New York: Dover Publications, 1969.

Schopenhauer, Arthur. *On the Basis of Morality*. Translated by E. F. J. Payne. Indianapolis: Hackett Publishing, 1995.

Schopenhauer, Arthur. *On the Freedom of the Will*. Translated by E. F. J. Payne. Indianapolis: Bobbs-Merrill, 1960.

Schopenhauer, Arthur. *Parerga and Paralipomena*, Vols. I–II. Translated by E. F. J. Payne. Oxford: Clarendon Press, 1974.

Janaway, Christopher, ed. *The Cambridge Companion to Schopenhauer*. Cambridge: Cambridge University Press, 1999.

Janaway, Christopher. *Schopenhauer: A Very Short Introduction*. Oxford: Oxford University Press, 2002.

Cartwright, David E. *Schopenhauer: A Biography*. Cambridge: Cambridge University Press, 2010.

Wicks, Robert. "Arthur Schopenhauer." In *The Stanford Encyclopedia of Philosophy* (Winter 2024 Edition), edited by Edward N. Zalta and Uri Nodelman. Stanford University.

Crone, R. A. "Schopenhauer on vision and the colors." *Documenta Ophthalmologica* 93, no. 1 (1997): 89–96.

Augustine on Good and Evil

Biography

Augustine of Hippo (354–430 CE) was a North African philosopher and bishop whose writings shaped Western thought on morality, metaphysics, and the human person. Born in Thagaste (modern Souk Ahras, Algeria), educated in rhetoric, and drawn early to Manichaeism and then to skeptical currents, Augustine converted to Christianity in 386 and was baptized the following year by Ambrose in Milan. After returning to North Africa, he became bishop of Hippo Regius. His major works include the autobiographical Confessions, the sprawling City of God, the philosophical dialogue On Free Choice of the Will (De libero arbitrio), doctrinal treatises such as On the Trinity and On Christian Teaching (De doctrina christiana), and brief works like the Enchiridion and On the Nature of Good (De natura boni). In these writings, Augustine forged enduring views about the nature of good and evil, the will, grace and freedom, time and memory, and the ordering of love that continues to influence philosophy and theology. (Confessions I–IX)

Before his conversion, Augustine taught rhetoric in Carthage, Rome, and Milan. His intellectual journey moved from youthful ambitions and Manichaean dualism to a Neoplatonically inflected Christianity.

The preaching of Bishop Ambrose and Augustine's own reading of Scripture proved decisive. In 386, after an intense struggle of the will that he narrates with unusual candor, Augustine experienced a turn toward God culminating in baptism at the Easter vigil of 387, alongside his son Adeodatus. (Confessions VII–IX)

As presbyter (from 391) and later bishop (from 395/6) of Hippo, Augustine carried heavy pastoral and polemical responsibilities. He wrote against Donatism (defending the unity and catholicity of the Church) and, later, against Pelagianism (defending the necessity of grace for healing the will). The sack of Rome in 410 prompted his decades-long City of God, a sweeping philosophy of history contrasting the 'earthly' and 'heavenly' cities. Augustine died in Hippo in 430 during the Vandal siege, leaving a literary legacy he himself surveyed critically in his Retractions (*Retractationes*). (City of God I; On the Spirit and the Letter 54–56)

Summary of Views on Good and Evil
Augustine's account of good and evil is anchored in three claims. First, all being as such is good, because every nature as created by God participates in goodness; evil, therefore, is not a rival substance but a privation (privatio boni)—a lack or disorder in what ought to be. Second, evil in the moral sense

originates in the will's disordered love (amor): sin is not ignorance alone but the misuse of freedom that prefers lower goods to higher ones, disrupting the right order of loves (ordo amoris). Third, providence governs history so that even the evils permitted are folded into a wiser order for a greater good. Across works like Confessions VII, City of God XI, and the Enchiridion, Augustine articulates how privation, disordered love, and providence hang together: the good is the fullness of ordered being and right love; evil is defect, disorder, and the self turned in upon itself (Confessions VII.12; City of God XI.9; Enchiridion 11).

Augustine on Good

Goodness as Coextensive with Being. Against the Manichees, Augustine insists that everything that exists is good insofar as it exists. Created natures are finite, but their being is a gift; hence goodness runs from the smallest to the greatest like degrees of light. God alone is immutable, the supreme Good, in whom there is no defect. To call something 'good' is to affirm its participation in being and its fittingness within the order of creation (City of God XII.1; Confessions VII.12).

Ordo Amoris—The Order of Loves. Because there are many goods, moral life requires a right ordering of love. Augustine famously writes that we are just when we love things as we ought—preferring higher goods (God, truth, justice) to lower (bodily pleasure, honor, wealth) and loving our neighbors in God. Evil choices reflect a perverse order: we cling to lesser goods as if they were ultimate, or treat persons—who should be loved—for use and not for their own sake (On Christian Teaching I.27–28; City of God XV.22). (noting some editions number this as XV.23).

The Will and the Good. Augustine treats the will (voluntas) as the pivot of moral life. Our will is good when it cleaves to the unchangeable good, and bad when it turns away. He rejects the claim that fate or the stars fix our choices: we are responsible because we freely consent to what we love. Actions take their moral quality from the orientation of the will—whether it loves rightly or is curved in on itself (On Free Choice of the Will II.19; III.3–5).

Happiness, Rest, and the Highest Good. The good for humans culminates in beatitudo—rest in God who is the measure of all goods. Temporal goods are genuine but insufficient; they are to be enjoyed in an ordered way as signs and means, not idols. The famous confession, "You have made us for Yourself, and our heart is restless until it rests in You," captures Augustine's teleology: true happiness requires the healing and right ordering of love (Confessions I.1; X.23–27).

Common Goods and the Earthly City. Augustine does not deny political goods: peace, order, and justice are genuine goods even in the 'earthly city.' Yet without reference to the highest good they remain vulnerable to domination and pride. The common good of a polity is measured by the order of love that structures it; a people is defined by the loves it shares (City of God XIX.13, XIX.24).

Goodness as Participation in Divine Order. For Augustine, created goods possess goodness precisely by participating—according to their measure and kind—in the rational order established by God. Proportion (modus), form (species), and order (ordo) are signs that a creature's being is a gift structured by divine wisdom. Accordingly, to affirm a thing's goodness is to affirm both its existence and its fitting place within the harmony of creation (On the Nature of Good 1–3; City of God XI).

Communal and Ecclesial Dimensions of Good. Augustine insists that the highest good is enjoyed not in isolation but in communion. Charity orders persons into one body whose common life is measured by what they love. Hence his famous political definition: a people is "an assemblage of reasonable beings bound together by a common agreement as to the objects of their love." This means the quality of any community's common good depends on the hierarchy of loves that binds it (City of God XIX.24).

The Dynamic Growth Toward the Good. Moral progress is, for Augustine, a gradual re-ordering of love effected by grace. Exhortation and effort have their place, but the wounded will is healed and elevated by a higher love, so that the good life is ongoing participation in God rather than a merely human achievement. Thus virtue is rightly ordered love sustained by grace, and hope marks our pilgrim progress toward beatitude (On the Spirit and the Letter 54–56).

Augustine on Evil
Privation, Not Substance. Augustine's breakthrough insight is that evil is not a thing but a privation: a lack of due order, form, or measure in a good nature. Blindness is not a substance added to the eye but the loss of sight; similarly, moral evil is not a created 'stuff' but the defect of will that deviates from the good. This dissolves Manichean dualism and preserves the goodness of creation (Confessions VII.12; City of God XI.9; On the Nature of Good 1–3).

Disordered Loves and Sin. Evil in the moral sense is the will's preference for lower over higher goods.

Augustine distinguishes use (uti) from enjoyment (frui): we should use temporal goods on the way to enjoying God. Sin arises when we enjoy what should be used, or use persons as means rather than loving them rightly. In this way, pride—self-exaltation—becomes the primal vice, bending the soul away from the common good (On Christian Teaching I.22–28; City of God XIV.13–15).

Original Sin and the Wounded Will. Augustine frames the universality of moral evil by teaching that the human race, in solidarity with Adam, inherits a condition of disordered love. Mortality and corruption are penal consequences that reveal the will's need of healing; this doctrine explains why sin persists even where knowledge of the good is present and why grace is necessary for true liberty (City of God XIII; Enchiridion).

The Tragic Bondage of Evil. Although sin is a free turning from the higher to lower goods, Augustine observes that such turning becomes a servitude: the soul curved in on itself repeats choices that diminish freedom. In his own conversion narrative he describes the divided will, drawn by contrary loves, until grace loosens the fetters of habit and pride. Evil thus appears both as culpable misuse of freedom and as a bondage from which we must be delivered (Confessions VIII.5–12; On the Spirit and the Letter 54–56).

Freedom, Foreknowledge, and Responsibility. Augustine argues that God's knowing future free acts does not cause them; divine foreknowledge is not coercive. We are responsible because we consent; the cause of sin is a deficient cause—the will's turning—rather than an efficient infusion of evil. The problem of evil is thus moved from ontology to moral psychology, without denying providence (On Free Choice of the Will III.3–5).

Physical Evil and the Wider Order. Evils like pain and death are consequences of disordered will at the human level, but Augustine also stresses that what seems an evil in part may serve a greater order in the whole. Predator and prey, decay and regeneration, even the penalties of sin, are coordinated within a providential harmony that exhibits divine justice and mercy. God brings good out of evils not by willing evil, but by wisely permitting it for greater goods (Enchiridion 11; City of God XII).

Grace, Healing, and the Re-ordering of Love. Because our loves are wounded, Augustine emphasizes the necessity of grace for the healing of the will. Moral exhortation alone cannot secure the good; the will must be liberated and directed by a higher love. Virtue therefore is not merely habit but rightly ordered love sustained by grace (Confessions VIII.5–12; On the Spirit and the Letter 54–56).

Comparative Section: Augustine's Influence on Leibniz

Privation Theory and the Nature of Evil. Leibniz's theodicy inherits Augustine's core claim that evil is a privation of good, not a positive substance. Where Augustine denies any independent evil principle and explains moral evil by the will's defect, Leibniz formalizes the point within a rationalist system: privations require no efficient cause, just as darkness requires no maker; they mark the limits of creaturely perfection. Leibniz repeatedly articulates evil as privation while distinguishing God's creative act (which confers all positive being) from the defects that attend finite natures (Theodicy §21; §30). Augustine supplies the metaphysical grammar; Leibniz embeds it in a systematic account of creation and causation (Confessions VII.12; On the Nature of Good 1–3).

The "Best Possible World" and Greater-Good Reasoning. Augustine maintains that God permits certain evils in order to bring about greater goods— that the order of the whole exhibits a beauty and justice that could not exist without contrast, correction, and redemption (Enchiridion 11; City of God XI.23). Leibniz develops this into the thesis that God chooses the best of all possible worlds: the simplest in hypotheses and richest in phenomena, in which the overall harmony outweighs particular defects (Discourse on Metaphysics §§5–6; Theodicy §120). Augustine offers the foundational idea of providential ordering; Leibniz generalizes it with the machinery of possible-worlds reasoning and optimality.

Kinds of Evil and Moral Psychology. Although Augustine does not present a trichotomy, his discussions imply distinctions between moral fault (sin), the penalties and pains that befall us, and metaphysical finitude. Leibniz famously thematizes these as moral, physical, and metaphysical evils. At the psychological level, Augustine's analysis of pride and disordered love anticipates Leibniz's emphasis on the will's inclination toward partial goods and the role of habits in moral character (City of God XIV.13–15; Theodicy §21; §241).

Foreknowledge, Freedom, and Responsibility. Augustine insists that divine foreknowledge does not cancel human freedom; God's knowledge is not a temporal push but an eternal grasp of temporal acts (On Free Choice of the Will III.3–5). Leibniz, confronting similar issues, argues that future contingents are certainly foreknown in God without being necessitated in the fatalistic sense. Divine knowledge encompasses the free choices that rational agents would make in given circumstances, preserving responsibility (Discourse on Metaphysics §30; Theodicy §§173–176).

Ethical Aim: Ordered Love vs. Rational Harmony. Both thinkers converge in aiming at an order of the good that integrates personal virtue with the common good. Augustine frames this as the re-ordering of love toward God and neighbor; Leibniz as participation in the City of God—a republic of minds governed by wisdom and benevolence (City of God XIX.13; Discourse on Metaphysics §6; Theodicy §135). The conceptual bridges—privation, greater-good providence, freedom under foreknowledge—show that Leibniz does not merely echo Augustine but transforms Augustinian insights into the idiom of early modern rationalism.

Simplified Summary

For Augustine, everything that exists is good in some degree; evil is not a thing but a lack or disorder in a good nature. We do wrong when we love lesser goods more than higher ones—when pride and desire twist our will away from justice and love. God permits some evils to bring about a greater order, and true happiness lies in a healed love that rests in the highest good. Leibniz later takes over this picture: he treats evil as privation, argues that God chose the best possible world overall, and explains how foreknowledge does not destroy human freedom. Augustine supplies the core ideas; Leibniz recasts them in a systematic, rationalist form.

Bibliography

Augustine. Confessions. Translated by Henry Chadwick. Oxford: Oxford University Press, 1991.

Augustine. The City of God against the Pagans. Translated by R. W. Dyson. Cambridge: Cambridge University Press, 1998.

Augustine. On Free Choice of the Will. Translated by Thomas Williams. Indianapolis: Hackett Publishing, 1993.

Augustine. Enchiridion on Faith, Hope, and Love. Translated by J. F. Shaw, revised. In Nicene and Post-Nicene Fathers, First Series, Vol. 3. Peabody, MA: Hendrickson, 1994.

Augustine. On Christian Teaching. Translated by R. P. H. Green. Oxford: Oxford University Press, 1997.

Augustine. On the Nature of Good (De natura boni). In Nicene and Post-Nicene Fathers, First Series, Vol. 4. Peabody, MA: Hendrickson, 1994.

Augustine. On the Spirit and the Letter. In Nicene and Post-Nicene Fathers, First Series, Vol. 5. Peabody, MA: Hendrickson, 1994.

Leibniz, G. W. Theodicy: Essays on the Goodness of God, the Freedom of Man, and the Origin of Evil. Translated by E. M. Huggard. La Salle, IL: Open Court, 1985 (orig. 1710).

Leibniz, G. W. Discourse on Metaphysics and Other Essays. Edited and translated by Daniel Garber and Roger Ariew. Indianapolis: Hackett, 1991.

Leibniz, G. W. Philosophical Essays. Edited and translated by Roger Ariew and Daniel Garber. Indianapolis: Hackett, 1989.

Adams, Robert Merrihew. Leibniz: Determinist, Theist, Idealist. New York: Oxford University Press, 1994.

Jolley, Nicholas. Leibniz and the Problem of Evil. Cambridge: Cambridge University Press, 2010.

Hannah Arendt on Good and Evil

Biography
Hannah Arendt (1906–1975) was a German-born
Jewish philosopher and political theorist whose life
and thought were shaped by the upheavals of the
twentieth century. Born in Linden, near Hanover,
she grew up in Königsberg and later studied
philosophy at Marburg under Martin Heidegger,
with whom she began a controversial personal and
intellectual relationship. She continued her
education under Karl Jaspers at Heidelberg,
completing a dissertation on St. Augustine's concept
of love in 1929. Her early academic work revealed
an enduring interest in the intersection of theology,
philosophy, and human action. Arendt's life was
dramatically disrupted by the rise of Nazism.
Arrested briefly in 1933 for political activity, she
fled Germany, first seeking refuge in Paris, where
she worked for Jewish relief organizations, and then
emigrating to the United States in 1941 after
escaping an internment camp in Vichy, France. In
America, she began to establish herself as a leading
thinker, contributing essays to major journals and
teaching at institutions including the New School for
Social Research and the University of Chicago. She
became a U. S. citizen in 1950. Her major works—
The Origins of Totalitarianism (1951), The Human

Condition (1958), and Eichmann in Jerusalem (1963)—cemented her reputation as a bold, sometimes controversial voice. The Origins of Totalitarianism traced the roots of Nazi and Stalinist systems, exposing how modern bureaucracy and ideology enabled previously unimaginable forms of domination. The Human Condition introduced her categories of labor, work, and action, distinguishing uniquely human political freedom from mere survival. Her coverage of Adolf Eichmann's trial in Jerusalem led to her most famous and debated idea, the "banality of evil. " Late in life, she began her unfinished magnum opus, The Life of the Mind, which explored thinking, willing, and judging as the basic activities of human consciousness. Arendt's intellectual independence often left her outside of philosophical "schools. " She resisted labels such as "existentialist" or "political philosopher, " preferring to see herself as a thinker engaged with the crises of her time. As a Jewish exile, a woman in predominantly male academic circles, and a critic of both liberal and Marxist orthodoxies, she forged a distinct path. She died in New York City in 1975, leaving a legacy of works that remain central to debates about freedom, responsibility, and the meaning of evil. (Young-Bruehl 1982)

Summary of Views on Good and Evil

Arendt challenged traditional metaphysical treatments of morality by grounding good and evil not in abstract principles, but in the concrete realities of political life and human action. She argued that evil often arises not from demonic intent or radical wickedness, but from thoughtlessness: a failure to exercise the faculty of judgment. This was exemplified in her account of Adolf Eichmann, whose ordinary mediocrity masked participation in extraordinary crimes. For Arendt, good emerges not from universal moral laws but from the human capacity to act freely, to forgive, to keep promises, and to sustain the fragile fabric of political community. Good and evil are thus inseparable from responsibility and judgment in the shared world of human plurality. (Arendt 1963) (Arendt 1958, 236–243)

Arendt on Good

For Arendt, the good is inseparable from freedom. In The Human Condition, she argued that what makes humans distinctive is the capacity for action: to initiate something new, to speak and act in public, and to shape the shared world. Goodness, then, is not simply obeying moral rules but engaging in the kind of action that sustains political life and honors human dignity. The truly good act is one that affirms plurality—the recognition that we live among others who are different from us—and contributes to a common world. (Arendt 1958)

She emphasized two practices in particular: forgiveness and promise-keeping. Forgiveness, she argued, interrupts cycles of vengeance and violence, opening the possibility of renewal in human affairs. Promise-keeping, by contrast, creates stability and trust in the midst of human unpredictability. Together, these acts enable freedom to flourish by stabilizing relationships without resorting to domination. For Arendt, they are not only moral virtues but political necessities, grounding good action in the realm of human plurality. (Arendt 1958, 236–243) (Arendt 1958, 236–243)

Goodness also arises, for Arendt, through judgment. Drawing inspiration from Kant's Critique of Judgment, she stressed that moral reasoning is not a matter of applying abstract rules but of imagining the standpoint of others. The ability to take the "enlarged mentality"—to see a situation from multiple perspectives—enables us to act responsibly and with care for the shared world. Good, then, is tied to the exercise of critical thought and the refusal to abdicate responsibility to custom, ideology, or authority. (Arendt 1978)

Another important dimension of Arendt's conception of the good is her defense of public freedom. She believed that the highest expression of human dignity occurs when individuals participate in the public realm, speaking and acting with others to shape a common world. In this sense, good is not only personal but political: it is realized when free people deliberate, debate, and act together in ways that affirm human plurality and resist tyranny. Political action is, for her, a kind of moral good because it sustains the conditions for human dignity. (Arendt 1958) (Arendt 1958; Arendt 1963)

Arendt also saw the good as fragile, something that must be constantly renewed. Unlike metaphysical systems that treat good as an eternal principle, she saw it as arising through ongoing practices of action, judgment, and responsibility. Goodness is thus not guaranteed by human nature or divine law but must be continually achieved in the realm of human affairs. This fragility, however, is also its strength, because it allows for creativity, novelty, and renewal in history. (Arendt 1978)

Finally, Arendt connected the good with resistance to totalitarianism. In her view, the greatest good is to safeguard human freedom against the systems that would obliterate individuality and plurality. The good is realized when ordinary individuals refuse to conform blindly, when they think for themselves, and when they take responsibility for the world they share. Good action thus becomes the opposite of thoughtless conformity: it is the courageous exercise of judgment in the face of pressure. (Arendt 1958) (Arendt 1978)

Arendt on Evil

Arendt's account of evil is most famously expressed in her description of the "banality of evil. " In reporting on the trial of Adolf Eichmann, she observed that the man responsible for organizing deportations to Nazi death camps was not a sadistic monster but a mediocre bureaucrat who insisted he was "just following orders. " For Arendt, the shocking lesson was that great evils can be perpetrated by individuals who fail to think critically, who retreat into clichés, and who surrender judgment to authority. (Arendt 1963)

This does not mean that evil is trivial. On the contrary, its banality lies in its terrifying normality: ordinary people, operating within bureaucratic systems, can commit atrocities without radical intent. Evil flourishes when people stop thinking, when they cease to question the morality of their actions, and when they refuse to imagine the perspectives of others. In this sense, evil is the absence of thought, a vacuum where responsibility should reside.

Arendt also distinguished between radical evil and banal evil. In The Origins of Totalitarianism, she had described radical evil as the attempt to make human beings superfluous, to erase their individuality and freedom through systems of domination. Later, in Eichmann in Jerusalem, she shifted to emphasize the banality of evil as it appears in ordinary obedience and thoughtlessness. The two are connected: totalitarian systems require the cooperation of countless ordinary people whose failure to think allows radical evil to be realized. (Arendt 1963) (Arendt 1951)

Finally, Arendt warned that the danger of evil lies precisely in its ordinariness. Because it does not require monstrous motives, it can spread widely through institutions, bureaucracies, and societies. Her diagnosis remains urgent: evil does not always appear as demonic hatred but as the everyday failure to think, to judge, and to take responsibility for one's actions. The antidote is not heroism but the steady practice of thought, judgment, and the refusal to abdicate responsibility.

Simplified Summary
Hannah Arendt believed that evil often comes from ordinary people who stop thinking for themselves. She saw this in Adolf Eichmann, who organized parts of the Holocaust but claimed he was just

following orders. For Arendt, this showed that terrible crimes can happen when people give up judgment and go along with the system. She called this the "banality of evil. " Good, on the other hand, comes from people acting with responsibility, keeping promises, forgiving others, and protecting freedom in public life. To do good, we must think for ourselves, see things from other people's perspectives, and act with courage. Evil comes from thoughtlessness; good comes from responsibility and freedom.

Bibliography

Arendt, Hannah. The Origins of Totalitarianism. New York: Harcourt, Brace, 1951.

Arendt, Hannah. The Human Condition. Chicago: University of Chicago Press, 1958.

Arendt, Hannah. Eichmann in Jerusalem: A Report on the Banality of Evil. New York: Viking Press, 1963.

Arendt, Hannah. On Revolution. New York: Viking Press, 1963.

Arendt, Hannah. The Life of the Mind. Edited by Mary McCarthy. New York: Harcourt Brace Jovanovich, 1978.

Young-Bruehl, Elisabeth. Hannah Arendt: For Love of the World. New Haven: Yale University Press, 1982.

Villa, Dana R. Arendt and Heidegger: The Fate of the Political. Princeton: Princeton University Press, 1996.

Bernstein, Richard J. Hannah Arendt and the Jewish Question. Cambridge, MA: MIT Press, 1996.

Benhabib, Seyla. The Reluctant Modernism of Hannah Arendt. Lanham, MD: Rowman & Littlefield, 2003.

Søren Kierkegaard on Good and Evil (Bonus Chapter)

Biography

Søren Kierkegaard (1813–1855) was a Danish philosopher, theologian, and literary stylist whose work launched the modern existential focus on subjectivity, inwardness, and the single individual. Born in Copenhagen and educated at the University of Copenhagen, he wrote under numerous pseudonyms to present differing perspectives on aesthetic, ethical, and religious life. His most influential works include *Either/Or* (1843), *Fear and Trembling* (1843), *The Concept of Anxiety* (1844), *The Sickness Unto Death* (1849), *Works of Love* (1847), and the massive *Concluding Unscientific Postscript* (1846). The core of Kierkegaard's project is to move readers from abstract speculation and "Christendom"'s complacency toward the passionate, responsible choice of becoming a self before God. His writings explore the dynamics of freedom, sin, despair, love, and faith with psychological acuity and philosophical depth.

Stylistically, Kierkegaard was innovative and daring. He employed pseudonyms to present multiple viewpoints, a method he called 'indirect communication,' which allowed him to explore existential questions from different perspectives. His writings combined irony, satire, parables, and profound psychological analysis, giving him a distinctive voice that bridged philosophy, theology, and literature. These features secured his influence on later existentialists such as Heidegger and Sartre, as well as theologians like Karl Barth and Paul Tillich.

Kierkegaard's personal life deeply influenced his philosophy. His broken engagement to Regine Olsen marked him with a lifelong sense of sacrifice and loneliness, themes that reappear in his explorations of love, faith, and commitment. He lived much of his life in relative isolation, often in tension with the established Danish church, which he criticized as complacent and worldly. His confrontation with Bishop Mynster and later attacks on Christendom expressed his conviction that authentic Christianity requires individual inwardness rather than cultural conformity.

For Kierkegaard, good and evil are not abstract categories but choices that define existence itself. He insists that there is no neutrality: to refuse to choose is already to lapse into despair, a form of evil. Every human being is placed before the demand to become a self in relation to God, and the weight of this decision presses upon the individual at every moment. Goodness means answering this call in faith and love, while evil means denying or evading it, whether through distraction, self-reliance, or conformity to the crowd.

Summary of Views on Good and Evil

Kierkegaard relocates the problem of good and evil from metaphysical systems to the drama of individual existence. He argues that the human task is to become a true self—a synthesis of freedom and necessity that relates itself rightly to itself by relating to God (*The Sickness Unto Death*, Part I). "Good," for Kierkegaard, is not a mere conformity to social rules but the earnest, faithful task of existing before God in love and responsibility; "evil" is not a rival substance but the existential condition of despair and sin that refuses dependence on the divine and misrelates the self (*Sickness Unto Death*, Part I–II; *Works of Love*, Preface; *Concept of Anxiety*, Intro.). He famously describes faith as a *teleological suspension of the ethical*—not an abolition of ethics, but obedience to God that may exceed ethical conventions, dramatized by Abraham's ordeal (*Fear and Trembling*, Problema I). Across the authorship, anxiety discloses freedom's dizziness and the possibility of sin; love of neighbor discloses the shape of the good as an unconditional duty; and despair exposes evil as a failure of selfhood requiring repentance and grace (*Concept of Anxiety*, Chs. I–II; *Works of Love*, I.7–9; *Sickness Unto Death*, Part I).

Kierkegaard on Good

Becoming a Self Before God.
Kierkegaard defines the human being as a synthesis of opposites—finite and infinite, temporal and eternal—whose task is to become a self by transparently grounding this synthesis in God (*Sickness Unto Death*, Part I). The good is not principally an external result but an inward truthfulness: to will one thing, the Good, in the presence of God. This interior stance does not negate ethical duties; rather, it gives them a grounding that rescues them from mere social conformity (*Concluding Unscientific Postscript*, I.1).

Faith and the Ethical.
In *Fear and Trembling*, Kierkegaard's pseudonym Johannes de Silentio presents Abraham as the 'knight of faith' who trusts God beyond the reach of finite calculation (*Fear and Trembling*, Problema I–III). The "teleological suspension of the ethical" means that the individual's relation to God is the highest task, not that ethics is optional. Faith does not license immorality; it transforms the ethical by anchoring it in radical obedience. The good is thus

fidelity to God that, paradoxically, returns the individual to the finite with renewed love and responsibility.

Love of Neighbor as Duty.
In *Works of Love*, Kierkegaard insists that Christian love is not preference or inclination but a command: "You shall love your neighbor as yourself." Neighbor-love is universal and unconditional; it forbids treating persons as instruments of private desires. This duty unmasks romantic partiality and social favoritism. Goodness is measured by whether the self is formed by the love that wills the good of the other regardless of advantage (*Works of Love*, I.5–9).

Anxiety and Education for Freedom.
The Concept of Anxiety portrays anxiety as the "dizziness of freedom," an ambiguous mood that reveals both the possibility of sin and the possibility of authentic choice. Anxiety educates by making the self aware of responsibility; in this sense, anxiety is not simply evil but can serve the good, moving the self from immediacy to earnestness (*Concept of Anxiety*, I.1–I.3).

Stages on Life's Way.
Kierkegaard's authorship sketches a path from the aesthetic (pleasure, novelty) to the ethical (duty, commitment) and finally to the religious (faith,

repentance, love). The hallmark of the good life is the transition out of aesthetic dispersion into ethical and religious integrity—choosing oneself in continuity and accountability (*Either/Or*, II; *Postscript*, I–II).

Truth as Subjectivity—Without Relativism.
His dictum "truth is subjectivity" means that the essential truth of existence lies in passionate appropriation, not in mere assent to propositions. The good is lived in how one exists. This is not relativism; the standard is the Good, God, and neighbor-love, but the path to this standard is an existential commitment, not a deduction (*Postscript*, I.1; *Works of Love*, I.1).

Kierkegaard on Evil

Despair as the Essence of Sin.
In *The Sickness Unto Death*, despair is the sickness of the self that refuses to be itself before God. There is despair of weakness (not willing to be oneself) and despair of defiance (willing to be oneself without God). Both forms are evil because they misrelate the self to its source and task (*Sickness Unto Death*, Part I.A–B). Kierkegaard identifies sin with this despair in the presence of God: a willful estrangement that prefers autonomy to dependence (*Sickness Unto Death*, Part II).

Anxiety and the Possibility of Sin.

Anxiety is the psychological prelude to sin because it discloses freedom's openness to good and evil. Where fear has an object, anxiety is objectless; it is the vertigo of possibility that tempts and educates. Sin occurs when the self succumbs to the temptation to ground itself in itself, foreclosing trust in God (*Concept of Anxiety*, I.2–II.1).

Offense and the Scandal of Faith.

The paradox of the God-man provokes 'offense': the mind's revolt against the claim that the eternal became temporal. To take offense is to harden oneself against forgiveness and grace, a specifically religious form of evil that seals despair instead of receiving healing (*Practice in Christianity*, I).

The Crowd as Untruth.

Kierkegaard warns that evil is intensified by anonymity and leveling: the individual evades responsibility by hiding in the crowd, which licenses cruelty without personal accountability. Public opinion and "Christendom"'s complacency are temptations to inauthenticity; the cure is single-individual accountability before God (*Two Ages*, I; *Point of View*, Preface).

Aestheticism and Ethical Evasion.

The aesthetic life appears charming but breeds despair: it fragments the self, erodes continuity, and reduces others to occasions for mood. Its apparent innocence masks the refusal to choose oneself in truth. Evil in this sense is a pattern of avoidance— endless rotation of pleasures instead of commitment (*Either/Or*, I; II).

Repentance, Forgiveness, and the Overcoming of Evil.

Evil is not the last word. For Kierkegaard, repentance is the passage from despair to healing: an admission of dependence that reorders the self in humility and love. Forgiveness in *Works of Love* is an obligation—to will the neighbor's good even when wronged—and a school for the self's transformation. The triumph over evil is thus not metaphysical victory but the daily practice of faithful love (*Works of Love*, I.9; II.5).

Comparative Section: Kierkegaard and Schopenhauer on Good and Evil

Chronology and Common Concerns.

Kierkegaard (1813–1855) and Schopenhauer (1788–1860) are near contemporaries who diagnose modern malaise with unusual psychological penetration. Both reject complacent rationalism and insist that ethics is about the formation of the self. Both explore suffering and the limits of reason. Yet their responses diverge sharply.

Good.

For Schopenhauer, whose metaphysics identifies reality as will, the good consists in compassion (*Mitleid*) that reduces suffering and, at its peak, ascetic denial of the will (*The World as Will and Representation*, I–IV; *On the Basis of Morality*, I–II). For Kierkegaard, the good is the task of becoming a self before God, expressed as neighbor-love commanded by God (*Works of Love*, I.5–9). Compassion appears in both, but Kierkegaard resists quietism: love is active, forgiving, and grounded in a relation that returns one to the world in responsibility, not withdrawal (*Works of Love*, II.5).

Evil.

Schopenhauer locates evil in egoism and the affirmation of will, recommending aesthetic contemplation and ascetic restraint as antidotes (*On the Basis of Morality*, II; *Parerga and Paralipomena*, I). Kierkegaard locates evil in despair and sin—the misrelation of the self that refuses God—recommending repentance, faith, and neighbor-love. Where Schopenhauer seeks deliverance from willing, Kierkegaard seeks the transformation of willing through grace. Both oppose cruelty and self-assertion, but Kierkegaard's cure is personal reconciliation rather than metaphysical quieting.

Freedom and Responsibility.

Schopenhauer views empirical character as necessitated, softening blame by appeal to the intelligible character's fixity (*On the Freedom of the Will*). Kierkegaard, by contrast, dramatizes the individual's responsibility in decisive choices before God; anxiety reveals that there is always a "leap" that no system can predetermine (*Concept of Anxiety*, I.3; *Fear and Trembling*, Problema III). The upshot is that Kierkegaard offers hope for personal renewal grounded in forgiveness, while Schopenhauer offers compassion and restraint grounded in a tragic metaphysics.

Simplified Summary

Kierkegaard says the most important moral question is how you exist as a single individual. Goodness is becoming a truthful self before God and loving your neighbor without conditions. Evil is despair—the refusal to be yourself in dependence on God—and the sin that follows from that refusal. Anxiety shows our freedom; faith heals despair; love restores relationships. Compared with fellow nineteenth-century philosopher Schopenhauer, who seeks to quiet the will through compassion and restraint, Kierkegaard calls for the transformation of the will through faith, repentance, and steadfast neighbor-love.

Bibliography

Kierkegaard, Søren. *Fear and Trembling*. Translated by Alastair Hannay. London: Penguin Classics, 1985.

Kierkegaard, Søren. *The Concept of Anxiety*. Translated by Reidar Thomte and Albert B. Anderson. Princeton: Princeton University Press, 1980.

Kierkegaard, Søren. *The Sickness Unto Death*. Translated by Howard V. Hong and Edna H. Hong. Princeton: Princeton University Press, 1980.

Kierkegaard, Søren. *Works of Love*. Translated by Howard V. Hong and Edna H. Hong. Princeton: Princeton University Press, 1995.

Kierkegaard, Søren. *Either/Or*, Vol. I–II. Translated by Howard V. Hong and Edna H. Hong. Princeton: Princeton University Press, 1987.

Kierkegaard, Søren. *Concluding Unscientific Postscript*. Translated by Howard V. Hong and Edna H. Hong. Princeton: Princeton University Press, 1992.

Kierkegaard, Søren. *Practice in Christianity*. Translated by Howard V. Hong and Edna H. Hong. Princeton: Princeton University Press, 1991.

Kierkegaard, Søren. *Two Ages: The Age of Revolution and the Present Age*. Translated by Howard V. Hong and Edna H. Hong. Princeton: Princeton University Press, 1978.

Schopenhauer, Arthur. *The World as Will and Representation*, Vols. I–II. Translated by E. F. J. Payne. New York: Dover Publications, 1969.

Schopenhauer, Arthur. *On the Basis of Morality*. Translated by E. F. J. Payne. Indianapolis: Hackett Publishing, 1995.

Schopenhauer, Arthur. *On the Freedom of the Will*. Translated by E. F. J. Payne. Indianapolis: Bobbs-Merrill, 1960.

Hannay, Alastair, and Gordon D. Marino, eds. *The Cambridge Companion to Kierkegaard*. Cambridge: Cambridge University Press, 1998.

Evans, C. Stephen. *Kierkegaard: An Introduction*. Cambridge: Cambridge University Press, 2009.

Ferreira, M. Jamie. *Love's Grateful Striving: A Commentary on Kierkegaard's Works of Love*. Oxford: Oxford University Press, 2001.

Kierkegaard, Søren. The Point of View for My Work as an Author. Translated by Howard V. Hong and Edna B. Hong. Princeton: Princeton University Press, 1998.

Schopenhauer, Parerga and Paralipomena: Short
Philosophical Essays, Vols. I–II. Translated by E. F.
J. Payne. Oxford: Clarendon Press, 1974.

Author's Intent

The purpose of this book is not to provide a single, definitive answer to the questions of good and evil. Rather, it is to recognize that every person carries their own perception of what is good and what is evil. These perceptions are shaped by experience, culture, belief, and reason.

The philosophers gathered in these pages represent some of the greatest minds in history. Each one struggled in their own way to define and understand the nature of good and evil. Their voices do not always agree — in fact, they often stand in sharp contrast. Yet in their differences, we are offered a rich opportunity: to discover ideas that resonate with our own convictions, and to be challenged by perspectives that do not.

The intent of this book is to guide the reader toward both recognition and exploration. Recognition — that they are not alone in their perceptions, for others have thought deeply about similar questions. Exploration — that by engaging with those who see differently, the reader may broaden their own understanding of human thought, morality, and the human condition.

If this book inspires you to seek further writings from any philosopher whose ideas echo your own, then it has served its purpose. And if it encourages you to wrestle with thinkers whose views stand apart from your own, then it has done something even greater: it has opened the door to growth, reflection, and deeper wisdom.

L.R.Caldwell

www.ingramcontent.com/pod-product-compliance
Lightning Source LLC
Chambersburg PA
CBHW060502280326
41933CB00014B/2833